Walking With Friends

Some Signal Mountain Walks

Jean Blair Dolan

WALDENHOUSE PUBLISHERS, INC.
WALDEN, TENNESSEE

Walking With Friends

Walking With Friends: *Some Signal Mountain Walks*
Jean Blair Dolan with Karen Paul Stone

Published by Waldenhouse Publishers, Inc.
100 Clegg Street, Signal Mountain, Tennessee 37377 USA
Printed in the United States of America
Editing, Type and Design by Karen Paul Stone
ISBN: 978-1-935186-83-0
Library of Congress Control Number 2017902811

   Personal notes of 101-year-old Jean Dolan featuring women friends who walked together weekly in the Signal Mountain, Tennessee, area between 1978 and 2017. Contains aphorisms, 35 watercolor maps and paintings by the author, and 59 color photographs. -- Provided by publisher
BIO026000   BIOGRAPHY & AUTOBIOGRAPHY / Personal Memoirs
BIO022000   BIOGRAPHY & AUTOBIOGRAPHY / Women
HIS036120   HISTORY / United States / State & Local / South

Jean Blair Dolan

To:

All those who love the great outdoors

Ten year old Jean Blair in 1925 with her cousin, Norma Gray, in their Girl Scout uniforms. The organization was founded in 1912. Jean is a Life Scout and became a devoted, active supporter of the program as a girl, parent and leader.

The Girl Scout Promise:
On my honor, I will try
To serve God and my country,
To help people at all times,
And to live by the Girl Scout Law.

The Girl Scout Law
I will do my best to be
honest and fair,
friendly and helpful,
considerate and caring,
courageous and strong, and
responsible for what I say and do,
and to
respect myself and others,
respect authority,
use resources wisely,
make the world a better pace, and
be a sister to every Girl Scout.

Prologue

Some women from Saint Timothy's were hiking on Fridays. I was pleased they asked me to join them. I hiked with them a while before I started these notes. They were Martha Crosby, Beverly Anderson and Peggy Collins.

Jean Dolan, 2016

~

"Have friends. If you cannot make them, remake yourself until you can. Solitude is a medicine, a healing fast, but it is not food."
Will Durant, *Mansions of Phil*

Hikers
Birthdays and dates joined

Beverly Anderson - July 20, before 1978
Astrid Andrews - November 1989
Gail Baschnagel - May, 2012
Ellen Boler - January 1981
Marie Braxton (King) - February 1993
Mary Broerman - May, 2013
Ruth Clark - May 14, before 1978
Ruzia Cleveland - April 1979
Linda Collins - December 1990
Peggy Collins - June 27(died 2001), before 1978
Jean Cook - April, 2012
Cynthia Cowan - Marc h 1991
Martha Crosby - before 1978
Ellen Crowe - before 1978
Sue Crowder - September 1986
Jean Dolan - November 12, before 1978
Debbie Fassino - July 19, September 2016
Jane Fry - October 1991
Nancy Fulcher - January 1998
Kay Gaston - November 27, January 1980
Karen "Mish" Gamble - March 2011
Diane Thompson Gray - October 28, March 1982
Gretchen Gugler - October 1986
Connie Hawkins - September 15, November 1981
Elaine Hill - September 1988
Hilda "Bitsy" Horton - June 2013
Jessie Hutchinson - June 19, February 2010

Jean Blair Dolan

Marsha Jenison - April 1979
Nancy (Clairmont Moughrabi) Johnson - December 25, January 1984
Gretchen Law - January 26, before 1978
Angelika Lingl - June, 2013
Carolyn Longphre - April 5, February, 2012
Pat Martin - December, June 1979
Dawn McCord - June 27, before 1978
Ann McKay - January 1991
Dianna Nye - September 1985
Pam O'Neal - before 1978
Helenna Ordonez - January 1996
Jo Ann Peliteer - November 1993
Margaret "Maggie" Popp - March 1995
Shirley Schofield - April 11, January 1959
Mary Seay - November 22, May 1986
Bunny Sedgwick - March 28, December 1994
Brooke Sedgwick- July 14, September 1995
Jane Smith - December 7 (died 2002), before 1978
Anne Marie Smith - June 27, before 1978
Karen "Narnie" Smith - January 1996
Karen "Pepe" Stone - February 29, January 1986
Lynn Talbott - January, 2005
Karen Thomas - June 1986
Linda Triplett - March 1995
Marilyn Truex - January 2, May 1981
Janice Younger - February 2, September 1988
Beth & John Weidner - May 2012
Wanda Wilbanks - April 1992
Jocelyn Willis - November 2014

Vagabond Song
Bliss Corman

There is something in the autumn
that is native to my blood --
Touch of manner, hint of mood;
and my heart is like a rhyme
With the yellows and the purple
and the crimson keeping time

The scarlet of the maples can
shake me like a cry
of bugles going by
And my lonely spirit thrills
to see frosty asters
like a smoke upon the hills

There is something in October
sets the gypsy blood astir;
We must rise and follow her
when from every hill of flame
Who calls and calls
each vagabond by name.

1978

October 20, 1978. Beverly [Anderson], Gretchen [Law], Peggy [Collins], Jane [Smith], Pam [O'Neal], Jean [Dolan]. Met at 9:30 A.M. Drove to Boston Branch outlet (gate unlocked). Saw hawks. Started walking 10:30. Arrived Chimney Rock 11:30; last leg approximately 240°; lunch; start return 11:45; arrived parked car 12:20; to Ladder Trail 14 miles. Sunny - warm

October 27, 1978. Ruth [Clark], Gretchen, Jean. Met 9:30 Gretchen's. Drove to Lay's corner. Walked to old strip mine - ruined 2 room sheet metal shack. Back to start. Walked to pipe line - down to Connor Creek; lunch in the sun; downstream to pipe line - up to start. Four dogs joined us. Drove to beginning of new mining road. Walked to 5 settling ponds and partially restored land of unsuccessful mining attempt. Sunny - warm

November 3, 1978. Anne Marie [Smith], Gretchen, Dawn [McCord], Jane, Jean. 9:30 Gretchen's. To Holiday Hodge-podge and on to strip mine site. Hiked down to Connor Creek up old road to another mine. Lunch at creek. Wine for my birthday; gathered weeds. Drove through Hidden Brook and went through house to look at mountain stone fireplace. Warm - sunny. Dawn came back here for coffee. Peggy and Pam selling weeds at Hodge-podge. Made $190!

November 10, 1978. Gretchen, Peggy, Bev, Jean. Walked from Anderson's. Perfect day. Bev found log covered with British Grenadiers. She served cookies.

Walking With Friends

November 17, 1978. Peggy, Dawn, Gretchen, Ruth, Jane, Jean. Met at Bev's. Drove to Halls Road, down to Double Bridges. Left to old cabin site (now new shack there) began to rain. I fell in creek. Retreated to shack for lunch. To cars - soaking. Pulled up small hemlocks to plant.

December 8, 1978. Jane, Ruth, Bev, Jean. From Sawyer Road along south side Marshall Creek - upper level. Crossed two streams. Went left at 3-way junction; went left at 4-way junction. Lunched at overhanging rock. Saw site of ruined cabin. Could see concrete and wire mesh caulking. Seems poor location for year round. Jane said likely a retreat. Got greens. Someone had cut hemlock and left it. Hunted for "BIG TREE."

December 15, 1978. Bev, Jane, Ruth, Jean. Clear 0° centigrade. Parked at end of Bates Road. Walked to pond, around house. Mick family rents there now. Fox family used the place in summers. Along trail to clearing we saw last week. New road down hill to flat.

January 5, 1979. Left at 8 A.M. Put wagon at Suck Creek picnic area. Beverly Anderson took us back to Peggy's. Charles and Jean Flowers joined us. (City High 1960, history teacher.) Pam, Ruth, Bev and I left at 8:45; across golf course; at Point 9:50 A.M. Down along ice covered cliffs. To car at 1:40. Light snow. Round trip in car 20 minutes. Five hours walk time = 6 hours total. This was Cumberland Trail first location. Trail went under the escarpment. Started down beyond Edwards Point through break in rocks.

1979

January 12, 1979. Peggy [Collins], Bev [Anderson], Ruth [Clark], Pam [O'Neal], Gretchen [Law], Jane [Smith], Jean [Dolan]. To end of Stewart Road. Asked Joyce Mayfield about homemade log cabin. Did not go over, but it's the young Lutrell - Jay and his wife, Alison Allen. We could see smoke was coming out of chimney. Logs cost 35 cents each. Walked to creek. Back up to back of Rankin's. Fire for lunch. Upstream. Beautiful cliffs, caves. Back to Mayfield's. Drove out to Jake's [Campground purchased by Pam O'Neal's family and re-purposed as home and organic farm] with Pam to feed horse; see their new log house.   Ola Mae Crumley died at our house.

January 26, 1979. Bev, Peggy, Gretchen, Shirley Schofield, Jean. Met at Bev's. Parked at Dolan's. Thru woods (box col) [A "col" is a notch or gap; in climbing terms it means a narrow crack, break, or crevice in rock.] to brow. Saw old [Girl Scout] day camp site. Fire, wine for Gretchen's birthday and chocolate. Back to Bev's for coffee.

> *Kneel always when you light a fire!*
> *Kneel reverentially and thankful be*
> *For God's unfailing charity,*
> *And on the ascending flame inspire*
> *The incense of your thankfulness*
> *For this sweet grace of warmth and light!*
> *For here (again) is sacrifice*
> *For your delight.*
>
> first part of a longer poem by John Openham (British)

Walking With Friends

March 2, 1979. Ruth, Bev, Shirley, Jane, Jean. Drove Don [Dolan] to Pipe Alloy, then we went to Dawn McCord's new house near P.Y.C. on Lake Chickamauga. Walked margin of lake over ridge. Back to house. Wine and cheese on deck with lunch.

March 9, 1979. Ruth, Bev, Peggy, Jane, Gretchen, Jean. Met at Jane's to Sawyer Hotel Spring. Still flows south of Sawyer Road. Through woods to large original log house. 3 small shacks full of doors and windows. Some large and expensive. Much lumber stacked and rotting. Daffodils. Around Long's Pond. Crossed to old hotel site. Sat in sunny meadow for lunch.

March 16, 1979. Peggy, Jane, Jean. Met at Peggy's 9 A.M. Drove to Prentice Cooper. Left Jane's car. Back to Highway 27. Left mine. Walked south of Cumberland Trail 1.7 miles to Lookout Bluff high over 27. Poplar Springs camp site. Beautiful sun. Lunch overlooking Tennessee River. Indian cave - interesting. Saw four deer cross road. Walking time: 1 hour to Lookout; total time 3 hours 20 minutes; 5.2 miles.

March 30, 1979. Bev, Ruth, Jane, Gretchen, Shirley, Jean. Met at Anderson's 9:30. To Sawyer Road. Walked in south of Marshall Creek on old road. Left beyond creek, beyond old cabin site. Lay in moss. Found mayflowers but not in bloom yet. Walked up a beautiful creek. Lunch. Dug a few daffodils in old pit. Very warm. Kruesi's property. We have crossed this property before, but not exactly same route. Same area as December 8, 1978. Found Mayflowers here several years back with Marian Nentwig's M. [mother?]

Jean Blair Dolan

To catch the freshened, fragrant breeze
From drenched and dripping apple-trees.
For soon the shower will be done,
And then the broad face of the sun
Will laugh above the rain-soaked earth
Until the world with answering mirth
Shakes joyously, and each round drop
Rolls, twinkling, from its grass-blade top. ...

The world stands out on either side
No wider than the heart is wide;
Above the world is stretched the sky,
No higher than the soul is high.
The heart can push the sea and land
Farther away on either hand;
The soul can split the sky in two,
And let the face of God shine through. ...

Renascence - Edna St. Vincent Millay

Walking With Friends

April 6, 1979. Ruth, Bev, Peggy, Gretchen, Dawn, Jean. Met at my house. Drove to Fern Trail. Talked with Evelyn Meeks. Followed bulldozer tracks through property being divided in 11 + 32 lots. Explored Little Rock City. Ate by creek. Dawn's birthday (April 15), but had her wine here [Dolan's house] No cork screw. Beautiful day.

April 10, 1979. Signal Mt. Dogwood Festival Trail Hike 10 - 3 Signal Point to Edwards Point. Ruzia Cleveland; Tom 6th grade, Skip/John Hertzing; Jeanette Dillard, Sam 4th grade; Ruth Clark. Cool, pleasant day. Started 10:15; back at 2:30; about 5.2 miles round trip.

April 20, 1979. Bev, Peggy, Dawn, Martha [Crosby], Gretchen, Jane, Jean. Walked from Bev's along strip mine to Middle Creek. Beautiful old still at creek junction. Upstream - old dam - ruined A-frame cabin. Ate in mid stream on rock ledge. Back through Timesville. Up strip mine. Delicious chocolate double tart and coffee at Bev's with her mother.

April 27, 1979. Bev, Gretchen, Jane, Peggy, Martha Crosby, Marsha Jenison, Pam, Ruth, Jean. Met at Falling Water (3 parking spaces there now) to Square Hole. Tried to find easier route. Martha fell. Climbed up to LUNCH ROCK. Through to Bates' place. Talked with Diane Mick, Sally Cook. Ate by pond; pink wild azaleas. Beautiful. Back to Falling Water.

May 4, 1979. Bev, (Gretchen got left at Payne's), Ruth, Joan, Anne Marie [Smith], Dawn, Jean. To Rocky Branch, through

empty lot to Service Branch. Followed creek by caves we saw on January 12. Found 2 lady slippers in bloom. (9 more after lunch on other side of creek.) Beautiful cascades. Off and on rainy. Lunch on wet rock. Back on other side of Hatfield Creek. Up to back of houses on Taft. Up unnamed stream to Rocky Branch Road, 3 lots from where we started.

May 25, 1979. Senior Day at Red Bank

June 8, 1979. Mother transferred from our home to Alexian Brothers.

June 15, 1979. I was canoeing Buffalo River with Ruzia Cleveland.

June 22, 1979. Anne Marie, Pat [Martin], Beverly, Jean. Drove to golf course. Walked to Rainbow Lake. Several tulip poplars have been cut. Vandals I believe. Upstream we ate lunch. Back to Smith's for lemonade. Anne Marie's birthday is June 27; Peggy's is June 27th.

June 29, 1979. Bev, Ruth, Jean. Drove to end of Forest Park to Falling Water. Picked up trash. Lovely clear, cool day. Back to Ruth's for lemonade and lunch. Jerry [Clark] starting porch and work room.

July 6, 1979. Bev, Ruth, Peggy, Pam, Jean. Met at Pam's [On Texas]. To Mushroom Rock. Celebrated Bev's birthday.

July 20, 1979. Pam and I found dead goat. Goat was a skeleton, chain around neck; locked to a tree. Neck bones pulled out of joints. Picked Butterfly Weed with rags tied on. This

Bev - Ruth - Peggy - Pam
Joan - met at Pam's

To Mushroom Rk.
celebrated Bev's birthday

July 20 - Pam + ♂
found dead goat -

— Picked Butterfly Weed
flowers with ragstied
on.

Found new road/road

N. SCK

M Rd   goat +
             x y + ⌃ +
     M   + x   escarpment

goat was a skeleton, chain around
neck locked to a tree - neck bones
pulled out of joints

was along Timberlinks on Prentice Cooper property. Peggy planned to gather seed. Someone else must have had plans.

> *Whatsoever things are true*
> *Whatsoever things are honest*
> *Whatsoever things are just*
> *Whatsoever things are pure*
> *Whatsoever things are lovely*
> *Think on these things.*

September 28, 1979. Dawn, Ruth, Beverly, Jane, Jean. Met at Ruth's. Signed a beautiful book, *Tennessee*, for Ellen Crowe "Remember Fridays." Walked in rain through new houses. Shirley joined us at Anne Marie's for lunch.

October 5, 1979. Bev, Peggy, Phyllis Reineisson, Pat, Shirley, Ruth, Dawn, Jane, Jean. Met at 9:30 Anderson's. To Roberts Gap Road. Down to first bend. North to overlook. Group got separated 5/4. Five of us to point. Four to old house site. Beautiful day. Met at cars 10 A.M. - 2 P.M. Flipper Bend area.

October 19, 1979. Pam, Anne Marie, Bev, Ruth, Peggy, Jean ___, Phyllis K, Shirley, Jane, Jean. Planned to go to Prentice Cooper. Stopped. Hunting season. So walked through Reflection Riding. Beautiful day.

November 9, 1979. Ruth, Bev, Jane, Shirley, Jean. Ruth had card [for opening the gate at] Boston Branch. Very foggy. Got lost going to Chimney Rock (GO R - THEN L) Back to Smith's in pouring rain. I brought wine for my birthday.

November 16, 1979. Jane, Shirley, Jean, and Gene Ryter. Left golf course at 9 A.M. One hour to Edward's Point. At bridge 12:15. We really walked and did not stop for lunch. Ate at end of bridge. We were on time; the major players were late. Sam Powell spoke. We were all on TV 12 at 6. It was dedication of new bridge over Suck Creek. The [original] bridge had washed out. Pam O'Neal came by car and took us up the mountain. Beautiful day.

> *The reward of a thing well done is to have it done.*

November 20, 1979. Peggy, Ruth, Jane, Dawn, Jean. Walked from new development off River Point along bluff to back of Shirley Miller's. Beautiful day. Saw 2 people on Edward's Point.

1980

January 4, 1980. First walk with Kay Gaston. [See narrative of this walk on following two pages.]

January 11, 1980. Kay Gaston, Bev [Anderson], Pam [O'Neal], Peggy [Collins], Ruth [Clark], Shirley [Schofield], Jean [Dolan]. Seven of us. Met at Gaston's 9:30. Drove to church on Mt. Creek Road. Walked up to W Road along old corduroy road [route.] Two hours. Lunch at Kay's. Saw two traps. Heavy rain all day.

January 18, 1980. Kay, Jane, Peggy, Anne Marie Smith, Beverly, Ruth, Shirley, Jean. Met at Village Food. Walked down Hollister Road across Fairmount, up North Fairmount

1980 Jan 4
Met at Andersons
Ruth. Shirley. Bev + I
To Gostons - + Jano's
walked to naturel bridge
EBS. marked in
rock
once part of area
dammed for water suply
thru trails + rock houses -
old strip mine area
(where Shirley + I walked
in snow winter 1977
when we explored
Caine House)

N To new Jolly House
To cane brake.
To Altuns- Pauls log
cabin. Back by another

route to nat bridge
+ Gustors - saw G.
what makes goats.
Lunch at Kay G s -
she told history of
E Bnow
her house is great.

First walk with Kay
Gaston 1-4-1980

to end. Turned right through gate to Marshall Creek and old Sawyer Road [that leads] to Sawyer Cemetery. Lunch. Walked back. Saw [Signal Mountain Methodist] Church steps, [Fairmount] Academy steps, and Fairmount Spring. Beautiful Day. [Kay Gaston referred the group to *Spring Notes From Tennessee* by Bradford Torrey to learn about Emma Bell Miles and the history of the area.]

Let us probe the silent places
Let us seek what luck betide us
Let us journey to a lonely land I know
There's a whisper on the night wind
There's a star agleam to guide us
And the wild is calling, calling
Let us go

Robert Service

February 1, 1980. Kay, Bev, Peggy, Ruth, Dawn, Anne Marie, Jean. Drove down 127 beyond fire tower. Parked. Took the oldest road [Anderson Pike] to the W. Left at highway to Sequatchie Valley. One hour down to farmer's barbed wire. Many choices [in trails.] We went down oldest. Up a newer, better road. Saw dead cow. Below 32° all day. Three hours trip, including lunch stop.

February 8, 1980. Bev, Kay, Peggy, Ruth, Pam, Jane Smith, Jean. Walk in snow over frozen ice. Met at Bev's. Out in Land Rover to Hickman place. Down old Anderson Pike 30 minutes on foot. Back to top. Drove down steep road and

back. Explored. Back to Jane Smith's for pit stop. To Jake's. Built fire in log cabin at lunch. Pam fed the horses.

As fuel is brot to the fire	*For I will tend to the fire*
So I purpose to bring	*Of human kind*
My strength	*As my fathers have tended*
My ambition	*As my father's fathers have tended*
My heart's desire	*Since time began*
My joy	*The fire that is called*
My sorrow	*The love of man for man*
	The love of man for God

March 21, 1980. Rain but met at Peggy's and picked up Shirley, Pam to Jake's. Walked to North Chickamauga Creek. Saw snake. Then down stream to branch. Up to Jake's and Pam's log cabin. Hot chocolate at Shirley's.

April 4, 1980. Kay, Jane (left early), Bev, Ruth, Anne Marie and Gordon Smith, Barb and Bob DeClarke, Jean. Beautiful sun. To Wheeler's Raid Cave. New tractor tracks, since Tuesday; horse buried. Hiked to height of land. Thousands of trout lilies, hepaticas - pink and blue; bloodroot; spring beauty; trillium sessile; bellwort; violet - white; one walking fern. At lunch, Mr. Cordell walked over to us. 83 years old. Said he owned 50 acres and had sold logging rights. Said we could dig anytime. He lives in Henson Gap. Turn right off Taft and right again.

April 11, 1980. Bev, Ruth, Kay, Jane, Dawn, Pam, Peggy, Jean. Met at Peggy's. Shirley drove nine of us to Prentice

Cooper parking. Took trail to Indian Rock house 0.7 miles, then to Snoopers Rock 2.7. Lunch in sun. Dawn's birthday and Shirley's so had two bottles of wine. Back to parking lot at 2. 10 A.M.- 2 P.M. round trip with lunch.

April 18, 1980. Met at Ruth's. Picked up Kay and Jane, Bev, Anne Marie, Dawn, Jean. Ruth drove. Took first road left (west) from Taft beyond fire tower. Dead cow. Retreated. I found yellow ribbon in a dump and tied around tree. Took next road and slabbed around, through poison ivy and wild flowers. Back up cliffs for lunch. Found road and old still and lady slipper leaves. Very hot and dry. Party April 19 at my house for Anne Marie, Shirley, and Ruth.

April 25, 1980. Peggy, Dawn, Jean met at Bev's. Met Jane and Kay. Drove to Creed Bates'. Walked to top of Falling Water then to Square Hole. Found one pink lady slipper in bloom, plus one pair of leaves. Beautiful wildflowers everywhere. Four hours round trip from the car.

May 9, 1980. Bev, Ruth, Anne Marie, Jane, Kay, Pat Martin, Jean. To end of Picket Road. The Spring property to Mike Creek overlook. Down old road to Suck Creek. Upstream to Lewis Creek. Up Lewis to 16 blooming lady slippers in one patch plus others. Most beautiful spot here on Signal. Slabbed up bank [south bank of Lewis Creek] to cliff. Upstream. Through break in cliff line to no name rock. Lunch. Glorious day. Total time, 5 hours. Moved slowly. Ruth brought wine. [See photograph on next page.]

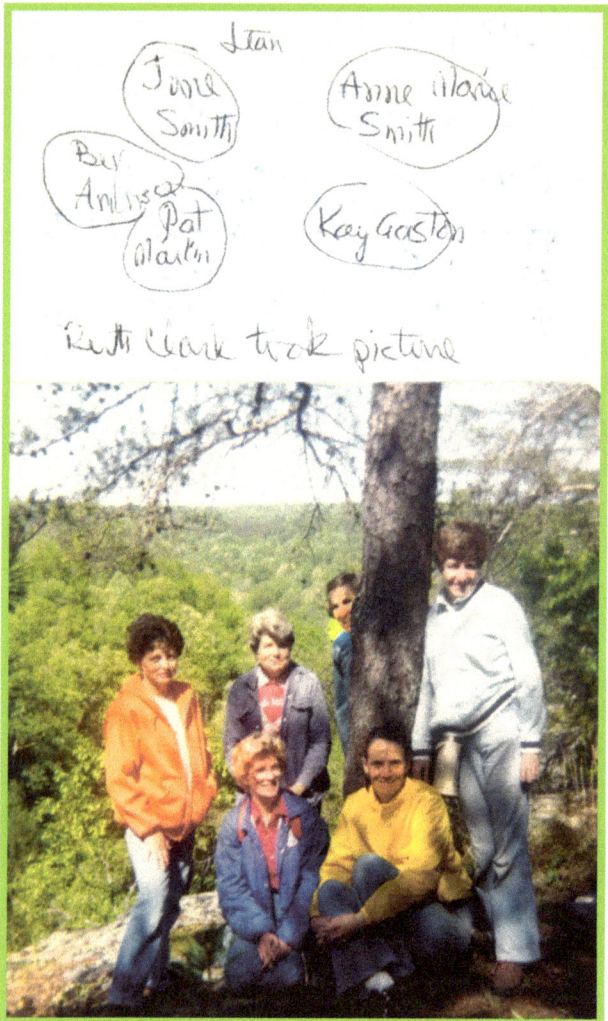

May 9, 1980 above Lewis Creek

June 20, 1980. Bev, Kay, Jane, Jean. Met here. Jane drove to Wild's driveway on Timberlinks. Found spreading pogonia = air orchid - near dried. Re-parked at entrance to strip mine off Lay's Road. Hiked into old strip mine; down to Connor Creek. Up stream lunch. Up to old strip mine with tar paper shack half down. Back through Lay's to car.

June 27, 1980. Peggy, Anne Marie (45) and Dawn (45), Jean. To Dawn's. Birthday. Talked and ate on deck. I made cake. Dawn made salad. Swam in lake [Chickamauga].

July 11, 1980. Anne Marie took us - Bev, Jane, Jean - to swimming hole in Suck Creek. Water low; trash.

September 1980. *Bev, Kay, Jane, Jean. Met at my house. Walked to Palisades Glen looking for rocks that could be called "Twin Sisters." We went upstream to Barrington Road then down, looking carefully at each cliff. I found a ring in dirt at the foot of the cliff. I thought it was a beer can tab. Ring was diamond set in platinum. No one ever claimed it. I gave it to Peter. Peter gave it to Jo Anne Alspaugh. We ate on top where we used to climb. To cave. Looked down and saw two similar rocks of uneven height. When we were below, they were equal. These must be the Sisters described in Jean Catino's letter. Back in dry creek bed to my house.*

[Kay Gaston, as a historian, conducted a great deal of research on Emma Bell Miles, famous artist and poet from Walden's Ridge. Kay published a book titled *Emma*

Bell Miles in 1986. Jean Catino was Emma's daughter and became a friend of Kay during the research process.]

> Ad sent to *Observer*: "Found a ring, in a rocky area on Signal Mountain. Nearly 35 years old. Identify. Jean Dolan."

September 26, 1980. Peggy, Jane, Ruth, Bev, Kay, Jean. Ruth here for weekend. Beautiful day. Cooler rain has refreshed many trees, although some are dead from lack of water. Met at Bev's. Mr. Anderson here. Got Caldwell's gate card to Boston Branch; park by pole D4421. Walked to Chimney Rock in one hour. At Boston Branch, trail goes north east. Walk: go 10° 5 minutes; go right; go left at road's end. In thicket look for milk jug on left; go beyond jug to left on old road. As road goes downhill and swings right, go left beyond plastic tie on tree. Find two rusty cans twenty feet apart. Continue to laurel thicket. Bev brought wine. Stopped at Sawyer's Spring on way back - dry.

October 4, 1980. Kay, Peggy, Jane, Bev, Jean. Left car at Edward's Point School. Walked old road to point. Lots more use. Point was trashy and Over the Road Vehicles had driven out onto rock disturbing the soil. Warm and lovely.

October 10, 1980. Kay, Jane, Bev, Jean to Mushroom Rock. Followed blue tapes then turned downhill. Ate on big rock in North Suck Creek. Upstream to confluence of Connor. Up Connor (We could see new road on right.) Turned up hill near nice cave-rock house to fallen oak with interesting

26

growth inside hole. Through escarpment near point. Two breaks in rock and cave. Walked south and picked up old road near Mushroom Rock.

October 24, 1980. Bev, Gretchen, Jane and I left at 8:15 for Knox. Picked up Anne Marie - to Montgomery to see Ruth Clark. Walked on Saturday P.M. to Indian Hills. Spitting snow. Ate at Golden Lamb Inn. Home Sunday. Got rick of wood for Jerry [Clark]. Visited Botsworth.

November 7, 1980. Pat, Bev, Kay, Jane, Jean. Drove to "House of Prayer" near Falling Water. Parked. Back through meadow; across broken down bridge; around hill to left. From dead end of road, go uphill slightly left to path. Go up path to right. Switchback. Follow under cliff line. Up through break. Left is south along contour line. Buzzard's Point. Colorful days; good wind.

November 14, 1980. Peggy, Jane, Bev, Pat, Kay, Jean. Parked at Smith's. Down Grey Frier Road across North Chickamauga Creek at Rice's Ford. Up along faint road. Through thicket to left. Met well traveled path and square hut (like at Double Bridges) Eight pieces of plywood. Found dried up pond. Peggy, Bev and Pat met Mr. Hickman and two others with rifles looking for hunters. Lunch in path. My birthday. I brought wine. Rushed back to Kay's at 2:30.

November 21, 1980. Bev, Pat, Peggy, Kay, and Jean met at Jane's. Across Corral Road to Marshall Creek. Passed old still, sawdust pile, and cleared patch in the woods (mari-

juana?) South along creek. Lunch in sun. Kay brought wine - her birthday. Back another way. Jane showed us two large patches club moss. Saw two hunters - one large white oak recently cut.

November 22, 1980. To Flipper Bend with Girl Scouts. Trenched to stop vehicles access. Many oaks cut and much trash. 10 A.M. - 2 P.M. with soup lunch.

December 5, 1980. Jane, Kay, Peggy and I met at Bev's. Through Sotere's to creek. Down through holly and hemlocks to Middle Creek. Lots of cutting; a survey tape. To Baptismal Hole. Lunch. Jane brought wine - her birthday. Peggy said Jill was being married Dec. 21. Back along old road now dead ending into Hidden Brook back yard. Across road through yards back to Bev's.

December 12, 1980. Kay, Bev and I drove to Toll House. Warm and Sunny. Met Jane. Kay had key so we went in to see. Tree looks great. To Kell Road end. Met Cartter Patten on road in 4-wheel drive rig. Walked across pipe line keeping right to old strip mine. Back and kept left to Connor Creek for lunch. Interesting trees we could not identify. Old house site; stone walled well. Two small ponds.

December 19, 1980. Bev, Kay, Ruzia, Pat, Jane, Jean. Met at Smith's. Bev drove. To top of Robert's Gap Road. Explored old house site and spring area. Ate lunch back from brow (too windy) in patch of partridgeberry. Explored rocky area. Cool and dull, but pleasant walk.

> *The only difference between stepping stones and stumbling blocks is the use you make of them.*

1981

January 9, 1981. Kay [Gaston], Jane [Smith] and I to Chicken Hollow Road. Much more ice and snow than our house. Explored old, small mine openings - warm air coming out. Several new strips partially re-graded. Through to bluff for lunch. Heard motor bike and saw tracks. Usual hard climb back out. Sun at times.

January 16, 1981. Peggy, Dawn, Kay, Jane, Bev, new Ellen Boler, Jean. Met at Bev's. To Horseshoe Road. Walked south through post-lumbering ugliness to creek. Ice 1.5" thick but water running underneath. Beautiful. To Double Bridges. Fire. Lunch. Back to car. 10:30 - 1:30. Cold day.

January 23, 1981. Bev, Jane, Ellen, Kay, Jean. Met at Kay's. I drove to base of mountain Godsey Road. Up Levi Gap Road. Finding and losing it through heavy brush to top. (Vacant lot at this time.) Ate lunch. Sun. Back down through brush. Delightful day. 1.5 hours up; 1 hour down. Cliff break is near Pearson's on Forest Park Road.

As our dreams are, so are we.
We shape in thought
What soon we shape indeed.
And what we daily hold within
We grow to be.

February 6, 1981. Ellen, Bev, Dawn, Jane, Kay, Peggy, Jean. Met at Peggy's. Started at new [Rainbow Lake] park entrance at 10:00 A.M. Old Girl Scout cabin site 10:15; to top of rock by lake at 11 A.M. Upstream crossed over log and turned south. Ate under rock above lake. 11:45. Half-hour side trip to 3 porthole cave. Down stream to bridge. Back to Peggy's at 1:30.

February 13,1981. We flew to Aspen.

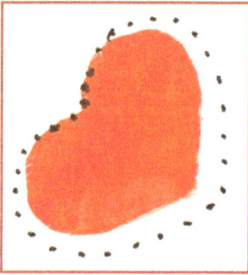

February 20, Group walked along creek Mabbitt Springs almost to Falling Water. Left car at circle.

February 27, Others down Marshall Creek from Sawyer Road.

March 13, I did not walk. They went up stream on Marshall Creek.

March 20, 1981. Dawn, Bev, Jane, Ellen, Bev, Jean. Met at Bev's. Parked at Cowboy's. Into woods to east along trail. Passed two swamps. Skirted Creed Bates' lake (improved waterfront) to Falling Water Falls. Lunch. Up hill to point over trail. To Square Hole. Up to Echo Point trail. To lake dammed on two sides (very dry.) Over hill to swamp. Back to Cowboy Whites. Walked at least 4 miles.

March 27, 1981. Jane, Ellen, Bev, Jean. Met at Bev's. To Sawyer Road north of Marshall Creek on old Murphy's Road. Down to creek beyond dam. (Kept close to creek for easier grade downstream until 12.) Half-hour lunch on

March 27, 1981.

March 27

Met at Bev's — Jane - Jean Ellen
to Sawyer Rd. - N of Marshall
Ck on old Murphey's Rd
down to ck beyond dam.
Keep close to ck for easier
grade - down stream until
12 — ½ h lunch on N bank

Walked down stream
on N bank until 2 rock walls
stopped us. A tree across
might give access to S bk
As we climbed up +
rested to could see gap —

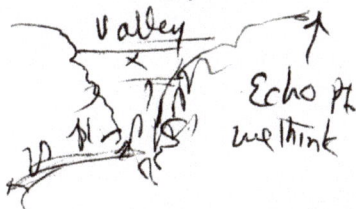

we found trail + headed W
only 8 minutes along trail
to Murpheys Cabin site.
2 PM at the cars. Dog did not
bother us as we kept to the
woods

north bank. Walked downstream on north bank until two rock walls stopped us. A tree across might give access to south bank. As we climbed up and rested, could see gap. We found trail and headed west only 8 minutes along trail to Murphy's cabin site. 2 P.M. at the car. Dog did not bother us as we kept to the woods.

April 24, 1981. Bev, Peggy, Pat, Ellen, Jane, Jean. Perfect weather. Met Jane at Cowboy's. We spent 2 hours for lunch and down to Square Hole up to Trillium Falls. Straight up to Echo Point; 30 minutes Echo Point to Cowboy's. Lots of water. Steep and dangerous.

April 28-29, 1981. Dawn, Bev, Peggy, Pat, Ellen, Jane, Jean drove to Gatlinburg. On Wednesday, climbed LaConte Bullhead Trail. Rain and fog. 6.5 hours to view sunset (none.) Had three room cabin with kerosene stove. Bed early. Thursday, sunny after predawn walk to Myrtle Point, Bev, Jean, Jane, Ellen. Down Trillium Gap Trail after big breakfast. Lunch at Brushy Mt. deep in sand myrtle shrubs. To the car. Drove to Rainbow Falls parking place and home. Seven in two cars. [See photograph on next page.]

May 15, 1981. Bev, Peggy, Ellen, Jean. Rainy. Drove to Vandergriff Road. Down back road to Jake's (O'Neal's.) Hunted for pink lady slippers. To Pam's cabin. Ate in pavilion. Tasted strawberries from the garden. Back through woods and WOW! There were 36 pink lady slippers. Back to cabin and home. Old 2-pen cabin built like Toll House with only chimney between pens. Nearly gone.

At Mt. LaCont April 28-29, 1981. Left to right, Beverly Anderson, Jane Smith, Pat Martin, Ellen Boler, Jean Dolan - on steps behind, Peggy Collins. Photo by Dawn McCord.

May 16, 1981. Jerry and Ruth [Clark] flew down Saturday A.M. Back Sunday A.M. The Gordon Smiths [Anne Marie] sold house.

May 22, 1981. Bev, Ellen, Peggy, Pat, Jane, Jean. New, Marilyn Truex. Picked up Jane. To Vandergriff Road, to Blue Hole. Started walking 10:15. Blue Hole 11:30. Waded; ate; drank wine - explored. Through blossoming mountain laurel and rhododendron. Beautiful place and day. Much traffic coming in from Boston Branch - 4 wheel drive.

September 25, 1981. Marilyn Truex, Kay, Bev, Peggy, Jane, Ellen, Sally W. [Wilbanks], Jean. To Chimney Rock. Ellen was visiting. Bev brought wine for her summer birthday. Beautiful summer day. Jane got key card from friend.

October 2, 1981. Sally Wilbanks and I ran shuttle (blue wagon.) Met at Peggy's. Marilyn, Bev, Jane, Sally, Jean. 10 A.M. when we crossed golf course. 11:30 Edwards Point. 2:30 crossing bridge. Lovely day but hike seemed long. Sally and Bev unhappy. End at Highway 27. We must have walked fast.

> *Let us then be up and doing*
> *With a heart for any fate*
> *Still achieving, still pursuing*
> *Learn to labor and to wait.*
> Longfellow

October 9, 1981. Bev, Dawn, Sally, Jane, Jean. Went to Brady Point. Met at our house. Scouted along bluff on top and below. Found cave like openings. Lunch at usual place. Turned up and through back yard on River Point Road. Turned down to highway and back to house. A lovely day.

October 16, 1981. Jane, Marilyn and I. Left cars at Village Food. Hiked along [Hollister] to Fairmount. Left on [North Fairmount] into woods and down to creek. Down stream (below Rankin's) Lundy Mt. Road. Bushwhacked back to Fairmount Road. Explored old cemetery. Stood on old steps to Methodist Church and Fairmount Academy. Light rain on return.

Jean Blair Dolan

November 6, 1981. Peggy, Kay, Jane, Sally, dog Rex and Marilyn, Jean. Beautiful day. Down Kell Road. Down to pipe line. Turn right into woods and down to Mike Creek. (Tried to check this one out years back.) Over to Serendipity Rock. (2 men, 2 trucks getting wood.) Lunch. Marilyn ate at lower level with dog. Warm in sun. Down under cliffs into cave. Up other side. Thought we were lost, but all home at 2:30.

November 13, 1981. Hodge-podge then to Kay's. Dawn, Connie Hawkins, Bev, Jane, Kay, Jean. Walked to stone bridge [behind Kay's house] through cane break, along pipe line. Kay went home. To Little Brown Church, along Brow. Ate in small terrace built long ago. I brought wine for my birthday. Cards from Jane and Bev. Little bag from Dawn. Found bittersweet on Clegg Road (Bluff Road in from Wilson) to Susan Yankee's new house; to Kay's; to home.

November 20, 1981. Bev and I met Jane at Sally Thomas' house on Sawyer. Through woods to Echo Point. Down. Very steep to creek. Right across from where we were on March 27. We went down stream and were at top of Trillium Falls. Exciting. We have been hunting for the spot for years! Lunch. Seed pods from witch hazel. Wonderful day.

December 4, 1981. Connie, Jane, Bev, Jean, met at Peggy's. Between golf course and Alexian property to Cumberland Trail. Explore Rainbow Falls from top side and bottom. Went down stream - up south bank to rocky recess in cliff. Found a violet in bloom. Up north bank. Ate on a rock. Up to Trail access, along under cliff. Found a passage up.

Walked along top. Found where girl fell off. Lots of survey-or's stakes. Picked vines, then back to Alexian - to Peggy's. Before the buildings were started.

December 11, 1981. Connie, Dawn, Bev, Jane, Kay, Marilyn, Jean to Flipper Bend. Explored old house site. Found well. Dug partridge berry. Wine for lunch (Jane's.)

December 18, 1981. *Jane, Bev, Jean. Met at our house. To Brady Point along cliffs back of St. Timothy's. Found large rock has moved with change of watershed. Tried to eat in woods. Too cold. Back to house. [See January 6, 1984 about rock movement.]*

1982

January 8, 1982. Jane [Smith], Bev [Anderson], Dawn [Mc-Cord], Kay [Gaston], Peggy [Collins], Connie [Hawkins], Sally [Wilbanks], Marilyn [Truex], Jean [Dolan]. Met at Marilyn's new house on Parson's Lane. Just next to field where we camped with Scouts (on Reynolds' property) to Sally Thomas' house. 10:30 at house. 11:00 top of Echo Rock; 12 Lunch at Falls. 1:30 back at Thomas'

January 15, 1982. Connie, Jean walked to Fern Glen. Lots of snow.

January: Kay into hospital Monday; Jane hurt ankle; Connie home - husband for surgery Wednesday.

January 29, 1982. Bev, Jane, Dawn, Kay, Jean. Met here. Parked at Ruzia's [on Signal Mt. Blvd. just blow sheer man-

caused cliff] and she joined us. Found old road - bridge found an old campsite on south slope - both sides Shoal Creek. Beautiful day. Jane fell and twisted ankle.

February 5, 1982. To Rocky Branch with Sally, Bev.

February 12, 1982.

Feb 12
    Met at Bovs. Connie
Peggy - Jean - Marilyn -
to junc of ck + Middle
(old still site) up stream
past ruined cabin - across ck
(+ old dam.) to rocky area
ate beside + ck.
    Hot choc at B. to Timesville
F —
    RKS
Old
Still
H.D.BR
Applend

February 6, 1982. Hiked around 4 ponds with bus. Paul, Joyce, Bob, Don and I. Supper here.

February 8, 1982. Bev, Marilyn, Jane and I drove to Birmingham, Alabama to see Ellen. Ate at Baby Doc's. Went to Garden.

February 12, 1982. Connie, Peggy, Marilyn, Bev, Jean. Met at Bev's. To junction of creek and Middle (old still site) up stream past ruined cabin. Across creek (and old dam) to rocky area. Ate beside F[ruedenberg] Creek. Hot chocolate at Bev's.

February 26 - March 5. Aspen

March 12, 1982. Bev, Jane, Dawn, Connie, Peggy, Diane Thompson [Gray], Jean. Parked near Miller Cove Road. North of Chicken Hollow. Hiked in along Peacock Creek looking for CAVE. No. Ate at creek. Someone getting mountain stone here. All in piles ready to load. Warm day.

March 19, 1982. Diane, Dawn, Bev, Jane, Jean. Parked at Chicken Hollow Road. Tried again to find [Saltpeter] cave. It is not where Stevens marked on the map. Found mayflowers. Ate at Lewis Creek. Up through Loret Farms; empty.

March 26, 1982. Bev, Peggy, Jane, Diane, Marilyn, Connie, Dawn, Betty Burton, Jean. Met at my house. Drove to mountain sign. Walked west side of Shoal Creek. Under bluff. Tried to get up through bluff to Brady Point. Missed it by 10/15 feet. Lots of poison ivy. Dawn's birthday. We had wine for lunch. Lovely day. Many wild flowers - Praecilia.

Jean Blair Dolan

Cumberland Trail Notes:

11 miles Signal Point to Prentice Cooper
Forest Wildlife Management Area.
Mullens Creek loop 11 miles
Start: One-half mile rect. rock = 4 bowls
Through rock and down steps - 1800 feet
Indian Rock House - .7 from start
Go 2.7 miles - turn north - view 4 pillars
Cross Sulphur Branch.
Side trail to Poplar Springs
At 3.5 Lance's Rock
Just before Highway 27, note rock bluff
with square hole 20 feet above ground.
At 10 miles Locharl Arch
11 miles to Signal Point.

April 2, 1982. Bev, Jane, Diane, Kay, Peggy, Jean. (Dawn
had p. ivy). Left the car near power line near Miller Cove
Road. (Bev and Bob Anderson came on Sunday with Mr.
Semens.) Down Peacock Creek along road to bluff. Down
through gap. Turn left along under bluff. There it is - Saltpeter Cave. (I was here, years ago with Martha Crosby but
did not have a name for it.) Interesting rock formation.
Lunch on top. Back to car. Saw owl. Pick flowers for Sally W.
Left car 10:10- after lunch 12:30 - back to car 1:50

April 9, 1982. Good Friday. Bev, Marilyn and daughter,
Peggy, Jane, Jean. Met at Bev's. To Wheeler's Raid Bend
(Dead Man's Curve or number 3 [curve on Hwy 127 north].)

Still Anemone in bloom; flocks. Found the Walking Fern. Back to Hall Road through the ___ yard (friend of Jane's) Large rock house just below. Down to Brock Creek. After lunch upstream to dump and through yard of ___. Dog bit me, but I was trespassing. Lovely day.

Prayer - Ralph Harper

Almighty God, if we have faltered because we are afraid, and if we are afraid because we have not faced the difficult tasks to which You are calling us, grant us serene confidence, quiet courage, and indomitable perseverance, that we may face the discouragement, failure, and even humiliating defeat in our endeavor to consecrate our bodies, minds, and souls for the advancement of Your kingdom. We pray in the name of Him who failed on Calvary, yet by his failure opened unto us the gate of everlasting life, even Jesus, this our Lord.   Amen.

April 16, 1982. Bev, Jane, Marilyn, Peggy, Jean. Looked like rain. I drove to Reflection Riding. Walked (free). Saw copperhead. He did not move when approached by us - just coiled. Saw ebony spleenwort and blue dogbane. They are getting ready for Earth Day tomorrow. (It rained.)

April 23, 1982. Marilyn, Bev, Betty Been, Peggy, Jane, Connie, Diane, Jean (8). Met at Bev's. Walked through woods to Baptismal Hole. Warm. Sunny. Old power line cut in terrible shape - from spray dirt bikes. A few plants struggling. Baptismal 1.4

September 17, 1982. Jane, Sally, Dawn. Jean. Walked to Buzzards' Point. Terrible chigger attack. All of us had dozens of bites.

September 24, 1982. Kay, Eleanor Goudis, Jean. Met at Village Food. Walked to Sawyer Road. Back through Cemetery.

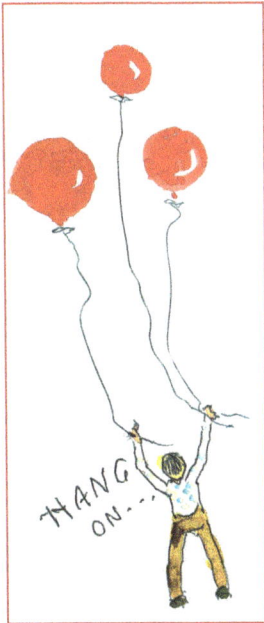

October 1, 1982. Bev, Diane, Jane, Jean. To Flipper Bend. Wine.

October 15, 1982. Jane, Diane, Jean. To Reflection Riding.

October, 22, 1982. Peggy, Diane, Jane, Marilyn, Jean. To Highway 27. Parked along Suck Creek. Terrible damage from **August 17 storm**. No trace of swing bridge. Jane found rock with fossil backbones. Warm in sun; not much color. [For years afterward, the group noticed residual damage from the terrible rain and mountain-top flood of August 1982.]

October 29, 1982. Library coffee.

November 5, 1982. *Dawn, Bev, Jane, Marilyn, Jean. Met at my house. Parked on Close property. Walked to Brady Point. Met James Shevlin and friend. They were rappelling down the Blow Hole and back up the route we attempted last spring. I went down top pitch and*

could climb back up reinforced with the friend's and James' encouragement. [**Jean would be 77 years old a week later on November 12.**]

November 12. 1982. Pat, Peggy, Marilyn, Anne, Bev, Jane, Dawn, Jean. My birthday. Walk from here in rain to Twin Sisters. Back for lunch here and wine. Connie showed pictures and talked about trip to Africa - daughter in Peace Corps. Deane came up for lunch.

November 19, 1982. Jane, Bev, Connie, Jean. Met at 9:30 here. Walked all around golf course - not a player. Ate at old picnic area. Home at 1:00. Bev drove.

December 3, 1982. Jane, Marilyn, Dawn, Peggy, Bev, Jean. Met at Village Foods. Walked down beside Harralson's back of Fox Hollow. Walked along old road by strip mine hole over/under rock outcroppings. Down a road with sign "No trespassing for any reason" and ate at a cleared area with dog pen, badminton court. Down along creek and back to new road that ended at Redd's.

1983

January 7, 1983. Bev [Beverly Anderson], Jane [Smith], Diane [Thompson] Gray, Sally [Wilbanks], Connie Hawkins, Marilyn Truex, Jean [Dolan]. Met at Bev's 9:30 A.M. Drove to Homestead Acres. Parked near Blanche ____ and through vacant lot to road. Saw two hunters and dogs. Logs felled over road to power line. Down and up to rocky outcrop.

Brow at 11:30. Moved slightly NE to lunch spot. Explored SW to top of lovely waterfall flowing from fault in rock. Out to point where we could see the full height of water fall – 80+ Two dogs followed Marilyn. Back another route – got lost – found ourselves. NOTES: "Hooty" J.H. White, 606 Bitsy Lane, 875-5136. Owns land NE of Buzzard's Point. Nov. 1988   Bob Long reported owner Buzzard's Point.

January 14, 1983. Beverly, Pam O'Neal, Diane, Sally, Peggy Collins, Kay Gaston. Drove to Sawyer Cemetery Road. Looked over the cemetery. One grave had dirt away from the grave; one could have fallen in! Turned right off the road. Walked down a graveled road past 2 houses, one left, one right. Thru woods; thru hole in rock, to brow. Found a marvelous rock to "perch" or lean against. Wonderful day for sunning. Walked out after lunch. Met landowner's son who asked us not to hike there because of hunters – which he didn't like! Bev charmed him, and if we return there need to invite him with us! (on his own property!) We stopped by Jane's place – Beautiful.

Sunday, January 16, 1983. Peggy, Gretchen. Drove to Anderson Pike near Redd's. Walked along new road; then left into woods. We found fascinating rocks. Named one double trouble. Back to car. Drove thru to Edwards Point Road, past Lay's and on new road from other direction. Very cold. Back to Gretchen's for a drink.

January 21, 1983. Ice & snow & slush and rain – no walk

January 28, 1983. Met at Bev's. Peggy, Diane, Jean, Dawn [McCord], Connie, picked up Marilyn and Jane on Corral Road. To Sawyer Cemetery Road; turned into woods below Needles eye Rock. Muddy and rutted to overlook; recently surveyed and cut; early lunch. Back thru pasture & inspected 2 cabins. Found glove. Back to road near tower. Jane and I explored all the rock outcropping back to Needle's Eye. Total time 10:30-1:30 lovely day – mud thawing. Dawn took pictures; turned out well.

February 4, 1983. Jury duty - didn't walk

February 11, 1983. Jury

February 18, 1983. To Aspen

March 4, 1983. Still coming back from ski trip

March 25, 1983. Bev, Jane, Jean. To end of Kell Road; down to Mike Creek; very high. Upstream to cross. Named falls "Right Angle Falls." Along escarpment edge to Serendipity Rock – another bridge to rock. Found neat sink hole with shelter. Lunch in sun. Much destruction from August 17 [1982] rain. Visible thru leafless trees. Saw bluets, mayflowers. Home at 2.

April 1, 1983. Bev, Peggy, Connie and I picked up Jane at Toll House. To Kell Road end. 10:00 A.M. Down to pipe line to North Suck Creek. Upstream until we could cross. Much storm damage [from August 1982.] Up Suck Creek mountain side to top. Walked NE. Found detached rock with 2 small arches. Too scary to jump over. Lunch in shelter.

Down to creek. Beautiful patch of pink mayflowers near slide. Upstream; crossed. Up hill. Found used trail never seen before. Three blue interesting rocks. Looked in Mike Creek gorge and walked S to pipeline. Car at 2:30 P.M.

Showers
of
flowers.

May 6, 1983. Met here. Jane, Dianne, Dawn. Park at new parking lot (Dedication tomorrow at 11 A.M.) Left car at 9:50. Down new steps that Don [Dolan] helped build. Followed blue blazes. Across stream (Middle Creek.) At 11 A.M. left path. Ascended to left, thru bluff to top of waterfall. Lunch. Drank Don's bottle of wine. Gorgeous! Along bluff to look-out. Back to 3 arch cave and down to trail. Met Mike Nentwig and 2 friends trying out their new backpacks. Across rebuilt bridge. Up blue trail to car. 9:40 - 11:00; returned to trail 12:30; at car 1:00 P.M.

Walking With Friends

May 13, Friday, 1983. Diane, Jane, Bev, Dawn, Connie, Shirley Anderson, and I. Met at Sally T's on Sawyer 10:00 A.M. At Blue[? or Square ?] Hole at 11:30. Lunch at Trillium Falls. Up to Echo Point at 12:35. Back at car 2:30. Steep. Met snake. Slid across Jane's arm, and she tossed it on Connie's head.

No walks in summer. School out.

September 9, 1983. Jane, Diane, Bev, Marilyn, Jean. Hot! Walked from Close property to Brady Point. Dry and hot.

September 16 & 23. I did not walk.

September 30, 1983. Diane, Jane, Connie, Marilyn and Jean. Wine for Connie's birthday. Chimney Rock. Beautiful day. Colors beginning.

October 7, 1983. Jane Smith, Bev Anderson, Jean Dolan, Ruth Clark. Cades Cove.

October 14, 1983. Dawn, Jane, Bev, Marilyn, Jean. End of Kell. Walked S of pipeline across Connor Creek to Mushroom Rock. Down to North Suck. Such water destruction! [Still from 1982 flood.] Up Connor. Steep on S side. Cross to north side-bank of cliff. Up through break. Hit trail (turned left.) Back to car. It took longer than planned.

October 21, 1983. Marilyn, Diane, Bev, Jean. Met at Jane's. Through woods to Hicks Branch Lake. Then downstream on

Winter 1983, at Jean's house, Ladder Trail. Left to right, Diane Gray, Ann Marie Smith, Marilyn Truex, Beverly Anderson, Jane Smith, Jean Dolan.

Pam's property to another creek. Lunch. Wine Diane's 40th. Cold and dreary. Took a quick look at Hodge-podge before a quick look at Butch, the Smith's steer, afterwards.

October 28, 1983. Jane, Gretchen, Jean. End of Kell. Met at Bev's. Down north side Mike Creek. Across North Suck (House now on Rodger's property.) Up to rock band. Found two-section rock house. Low area for sleeping, high area for cooking. Lunch. Found perfect hornets' nest. Bev took for school. Found an active still. Back across North Suck Creek up to interesting rocks, to pipeline, to Kell Road extension, to cars.

November 4, 1983. Peggy, Joel Solomon and girl friend, Pam, Diane, Jane, Connie, Jean. Chimney Rock. Fog - damp. Joel played his pipe right out of middle ages.

November 11, 1983. Birthday. To pipe line bluff. Dawn, Jane, Jean, __, __. Got lost.

November 18, 1983. Anne Marie, Connie, Jane. Walked to Pipe Line bluff. Jane put Connie in charge of direction. [This was a big joke with the group, because Connie had absolutely no sense of direction. She very frequently said about a place she had been dozens of times, "This looks sort of familiar. Have we been here before?"]

November 25, 1983. Friday after Thanksgiving. No walk.

Angels We Have Heard On High

December 2, 1983. Anne Marie and sister-in-law, Connie, Jane, Jean. Left car beside Brown's Chapel. Walked to bluff beyond Johnson Spring. Cold wind. Nice rock area near spring. To Mole Hill Pottery on way home, Anne Marie to hospital; that night! APPENDIX.

December 11, 1983. Jane's birthday. Off Sawyer Cemetery Road to bluff. Found waterfall and old still site. Sunny and warm. Wine.

December 16, 1983. Jane and I parked at her house. I got some club moss for decoration. To Marshal Creek. Across up to end of North Fairmount Road and new house. Pipe Line? Cold.

1984

January 6, 1984. Jane [Smith], Nancy Moughrabi, Anne Marie [Smith], Connie [Hawkins], Marilyn [Truex], Jean [Dolan]. Met at my house. Cold but sunny and getting warmer. Down Cherokee Lane to park. Scrambled under dump and Saint Timothy's [Episcopal Church] to sewer line. Check rock. It has not moved. [See December 18, 1981 about rock movement.] Slot too narrow for a flat hand to pass between tree and rock. Skirted under bluff. Up into Powell's yard. Lunch up hill from new road. Back up Shoal Creek Road closed to cars because of ice. Very pleasant.

January 13, 1984. No walk.

February 17 - reminder library

March 16 - Aspen - no walk

March 30, 1984. I picked up Jane at her house. We parked on Vandergriff Road. To Blue Hole with detour to right at old house site. Trail faded. Used a Bee Line. Found old path, a fence, & came out on the road to Power Line. Down the line into the woods to the creek. Lots of trash but still beautiful. Ate near water but terrain changed since storm of August 1982. Back to car. Took a quick look at Anne Marie's house. We walked about 4.5 - 5 miles.

April 4, 1984. Jane, Nancy, Dawn, Jean. To Reflection Riding. A perfect day.

Summer pause – no walks

A rainbow - my symbol for my
happiness!

September 14, 1984. Rappelled off Brady Point

September 21, 1984. Jane, Sherrie [Dolan], Jean. End of road.

October 5, 12, 19, 26 - out of town

November 2, 1984. Home from Frankfort

November 9, 1984. No walk

November 16, 1984. Jane, Connie, Nancy, Jean. Left car at Sally Thomas Worland's. Thru to Lunch Rock (Echo Point.) Down slide (to W) new since we were last here. Perhaps rain of August 1982. [So much rain fell that a flood dislodged huge boulders in creeks and washed out the bridge on Suck Creek. The hikers thereafter referred to "the flood of 1982."] Two beautiful falls in creek and one small from Buzzards' Point side. Much water. We could cross with difficulty. Cold day but delightful in sun. Still lovely color in deciduous trees. Lunch in a saddle. My birthday. Cranberry wine from Plymouth (Commonwealth Winery.) Back up ridge. Beautiful day.

November 23, 1984. - No walk

December 14, 1984. Dawn, Jane, and I walked along Marshall Creek. Cold. Beautiful. Dawn took pictures of ice. Cold. Started late.

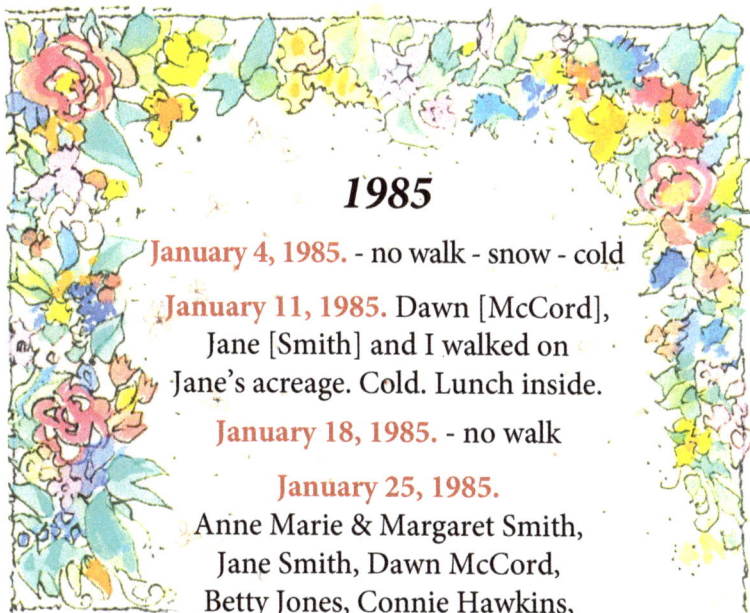

1985

January 4, 1985. - no walk - snow - cold

January 11, 1985. Dawn [McCord], Jane [Smith] and I walked on Jane's acreage. Cold. Lunch inside.

January 18, 1985. - no walk

January 25, 1985.
Anne Marie & Margaret Smith,
Jane Smith, Dawn McCord,
Betty Jones, Connie Hawkins,
Jean Dolan. Left van near Sawyer Cemetery Road through woods to Roberts Gap Road. Lots of ice. Lunch on big rock. Margaret Smith going to New York for job interview. (Did not get it.)

February 1, 1985. At Hawkins party for McCord. Went with Robin Holt. Home from Raleigh.

February 8, 1985. Connie, Jane, Nancy, Dawn, Jean. To New Hassler Road. Hiked to Mushroom Rock and toward

Edward's Point. Lunch in rocky dell. Found a few old blue blazes. Back through woods to road.

February 10, 1985. Sunday P.M. Marilee Stites and Gary Cox. CISV. Walk from Edward's Point School to Edward's Point. Turned right. Followed old trail one hour along escarpment then turned right up grade to old house site. Back to car. Total time 2 P.M. to 5 P.M. Three hours to Sportsman's Club (Old Edward's Point School) and return.

February 22 - March 1 - March 8 - Aspen

March 15, 1985. Dawn, Jane, Jean. Picked up Jane. Left car above Sawyer Cemetery and through woods to old hunting shacks. To overlook Point. North along old road to Rocky Branch. Downhill. Lovely cascade. Out to Roberts Gap Road. Up to cutoff. Back to Sawyer Cemetery.

March 22, 1985. Dawn McCord and mother Mrs. Fern, Diane, Nancy, Jane and I here. Dawn showed pictures. Lunch. Rainy outside.

March 29, 1985. Jane, Diane Thompson Gray, came here. To Walden Sport Club. Walk to old house place. Turned right down steep road to large strip mine area. Through to bluff. Turned left along bluff. Crossed two streams. Also saw tanager, one large, and one small snake. Saw many trailing arbutus in bloom - white and pink. To Edward's Point. Back to car. Car to car 10 A.M. - 2:30.

April 5, 1985. Hornigs here

Jean Blair Dolan

April 12, 1985. Jane, Nancy and I tried to get down bluff off Palisades. Too steep. Tried "Doggy Hole." I could. They didn't want to try. A development project below bluff from Dr. Winder's to Soloff's. Beautiful day. Met Mrs. Price - lives beside Doggy Hole (on Town property.) Ate at Signal Point. NOTE: February 2000. Development turned out to be B.J. Watson. There is a lot of grading, pieces of equipment, but no house yet. There is a trailer sometimes where B.J.'s father and mother live.

April 19, 1985. Jane, Bev, Connie, Nancy and I to Buzzard's Point from Sawyer Cemetery Road. Beautiful day.

April 20, 1985. Volks march. We wrote to Dawn and Shirley. Sometime after this, Nancy and I drove to Majestic Views subdivision and hiked to under bluff, south. Found much trash. Caves used by children and finally to Doggy Hole. Majestic Views access from Taft at big curve.

Summer pause – no walks

September 13, 1985. Jane and Connie and I drove to Suck Creek Road and walked along damage of slide. Then along creek looking for trail. Home early.

September 20, 1985. Anne Marie, Connie, Marilyn, Diana Nye, Jane, Betty Jones, Jean. Walked from Jane's all around Jake's [A summer camp that had operated for many years but was closed and land sold to O'Neal family.] The O'Neals are digging out one pond and rebuilding dam. We had lunch on corner of log cabin's porch. Five miles. Anne Marie and I got terrible chiggers.

September 27, 1985. Jane, Marilyn, Jean. Parked off Taft on Chicken Hollow Road. Red survey marks. To Saltpeter Cave (Turn left at point where road curves right.) Walked three hours - at least 5 miles. Lunch in the sun. Long, hard back up. Rock formations below secondary bluff interesting. Lewis Creek was damaged August 1982.

October 5, 1985. Jane, Marilyn, Jean. Marilyn came by here at 10:15 and picked up Jane at 10:30. Started walking at 10:45. (Take two routes of Flipper Bend path.) Saw three men returning as we approached the end at bluff. Lunch 11:45-12:15. Side trip to old house site. Inspected spring, well. Side trip to rocks. Back to car at 1:30. Beautiful afternoon after foggy AM through lunch. Shirt sleeves.

October 12, 1985. Marilyn, Connie, Diana, Jane, Pat Martin, Nancy, Jean. To Edwards Point School. Walked to campsite on BS Trail to point (before Edwards) for lunch. One hour twenty minutes. Back on road. Beautiful day. Dry. One hour.

October 18, 1985. Jane, Dianna Nye, Pat Martin, Maria Lubkowitz, Marilyn, Jean. Met at Jane's. Drove to Mill Creek Road (Homestead Acres). Walk to Powerline Overlook, south to lunch place. Dry. (Note waterfall and grotto above.) Yellow jackets everywhere. Found another road that needs following. One hour in. One hour 15 minutes out.

November 15, 1985. Buzzard's Point. My birthday.

December 6, 1985. Mushroom Rock almost. No walks until January 3rd. Over for 1985.

1986

January 3, 1986. Marilyn [Truex], Dianna [Nye], Jane [Smith], Beverly [Anderson], Karen [Stone], Jean [Dolan]. To Flipper Bend. Karen Stone walked with us for the first time. Two bottles of wine. Cold. Sunny.

January 10, 1986. Diana, Karen, Maria and Daphne Lubkowitz, Anne Marie Smith, Jane Smith, Nancy Moughrabi, Jean. Drove to Prentice Cooper Trail Parking (in Prentice Cooper Forest.) Started hiking 10:15. Non trail. Lunch at 11:45. Start back 12:30; at van 1:45. About 15 minutes drive.

January 17, 1986. Jane, Nancy, Jean. Met 9:30 at Toll House. Parked at end of Kell Road. Across North Suck up hill to lunch rock. (We ate here a few years back.) Up steam to old road under Rogers property. Forest fire damage.

January 24, 1986. Jane, Connie, Maria, Jean. Met at my house. Parked at end of road beyond Edward's Point School.

Happiness is...

10-11:30 to Mushroom Rock. Lunch. Back at car 1:30. Very good loop. Mostly on old strip mine roads.

January 31, 1986. To Falling Water. I did not walk.

February 7, 1986. Connie, Maria, Karen, Jean. Met at Hawkins'. Drove to Edward's Point School in Karen's Jeep. Left school 10 AM. Twenty minutes to old house site and turn off through woods. Along bluff to Edward's Point. 11:45 lunch on route. Could see new house between Alexian and Signal Point. Back along road to school. 1:00 PM.

Sunday: Star Tenders walk. Same as February. Buz Jones, Carol Buris, Don & Jean Dolan, Bob & Joyce Merritt, Paul & Evelyn Gaber. McNabbs, Brandfasts, Wilsons, and Kelly joined us at supper.

February 14, 1986. Too icy to walk.

February 21 - 28 - March 7. We were in Aspen.

March 14, 1986. Jane, Karen, Maria, Jean. Met at Jane's. Hiked in rain to Marshall Creek. Karen was 43 so brought wine.

March 21, 2016. Bev, Jane, Karen, Maria, and Daphne Maria's daughter, and myself. Met here. To Rainbow Lake area. Could not cross creek upstream so back to bridge. Up to twin caves for lunch. Cool and Sunny. 10:00-1:00. Old Girl Scout Cabin torn down.

March 28, 1986. Maria, Jane and I to Mushroom Rock from end of Kell Road.

April 25, 1986 at Roan Mountain with two unidentified through-hikers are, left to right, Jane Smith, Beverly Anderson, Jean Dolan, and Marilyn Truex. The photo was taken by Gretchen Law.

April 4, 1986. Reflection Riding.

April 11, 1986. Don and I with Choto at Rugby [Old English experimental utopian settlement on Cumberland Plateau in Morgan County, Tennessee]

April 25, 1986. Jane, Bev, Marilyn, Gretchen and I to Roan Mountain State Park.

May 2, 1986. Margaret and I had picnic at PXC. Watkins to Serendipity Rock.

May 9, 1986. Connie and friend Barb ___, Karen and I to Dog Hole. Parked at Lays. Got lost. Too steep. Beautiful laurel and rhododendron blooms. Ate at Echo Point.

May 16, 1986. Jane, Karen, and I met at Anne Marie's. Looked at laurel. Down to rock bridge. To Gaston's. Kay took us in her expanded cabin. Beautiful. Copper gutters. Lunch. Through culvert [under East Brow Road to Cascade Falls] between Caine's and Yankee's.

May 23, 1986. Jane, Bev, Nancy, Karen, Mary Seay (new hiker), Marta Fockler, Jean. Parked on Hixson Camp Road. Through old trails to Blue Hole. Beautiful laurel and rhododendron. New damage by dirt bikes. Trash. Warm fire. Saw three boys on vehicles. Two 2-wheelers, one 4-wheeler. Yellow lady slippers.

May 30, 1986. Bev, Jane, Karen, Mary, Anne Marie, and I. Met at bridge Sawyer Road. Along Sawyer side Marshall Creek. Beautiful. Found turtles. Laurel and rhododendron

just past peak bloom. Lots of water in creek. Fish. Beaver have been eating trees.

June 6, 1986. Jane, Dawn McCord, Maria, ___ , and I met at Sawyer Cemetery. Karen Stone did not meet us. Had gone to wrong cemetery, but we met her at Sawyer Road by chance. She was on way to right cemetery and crossed path. Signs all over where we walked last week. Hot.

June 13, 1986. Marilyn Harbaugh here. Walked to Serendipity Rock. Karen Thomas. Drove to Karen's to swim.

June 29, 1986. Party at Truex [home]. Maria & Axil [Lubkowitz]; Sonja & Mike (Pickering?); Jean & Don [Dolan], Bev & Paul [Anderson], Anne Marie & Gordon [Smith], Karen & Charlie [Stone], Karen & John [Thomas], Jane & Joe [Smith]

July 11, 1986. Swam in Karen Thomas' pool.

Summer pause

September 12, 1986. Jane, Maria, Karen Stone, Jean. Parked near Majestic Views. Hiked up to foot of Doggie Hole. Found small coal diggings. One lake dried up.

September 19, 1986. *To Karen Stone's for brunch with Mrs. [Martha] McCoy.*

September 27, 1986. Nancy, Jane, Maria, Diane, Mary Seay, Karen, Jean. Met here. Hiked to Edward's Point along road. Hot.

October 3, 1986. New Edward's Point trail

October 27, 1986. Jane, Mary, Gretchen, Karen, Jean. Swim at Boston Branch Lake.

October 24, 1986. Jane and I to brow in the rain.

October 31, 1986. Halloween - no hike

November 14, 1986. Jane, Maria, Karen Stone and I. SUN! Birthday hike. Buzzard's Point. From point to Roberts Gap Road, back to Sawyer Cemetery Road.

November 21, 1986. Karen, Connie, Dianna, Jane, Jean. Under bluff north from Ford Gap.

November 28, 1986. No group hike, but Emerson, Pete Dolans and us [Don & Jean Dolan] Signal Point to Rainbow Lake.

December 5, 1986. Jane's birthday. Connie, Karen Stone, Jane, Maria, Marilyn, Jean. To Echo Point. To creek. Could not get to top of falls. Ate in sunny spot.

December 12, 1986. Marilyn, Karen, Jean. SNOW. Parked at Middle Creek and Edwards Point Road 10 AM. Up left side Stanley Creek until we could cross. To boundary of Prentice Cooper. Found Silver Bells, lot

markers. To Middle Creek. Ate at cascade. Began to snow. Back right side of Middle Creek to Freudenberg [Creek]. Upstream until we could cross. Down to Middle Creek Road. Look at houses. Car at 12:45.

December 19, 1986. Walked.

1987

January 2, 1987. Beverly [Anderson], Marilyn [Truex], Karen [Stone], Jane [Smith], Maria [Lubkowitz], Jean [Dolan]. Parked at Jane's mother's, Cookie Parker. We had wine for Marilyn's birthday. Explored rocks in back of Bachman School.

Thanksgiving luncheon at home of Beverly Anderson. Left to right, Beverly, Jane Smith, Ellen Boler, Jean Dolan, Anne Marie Smith, Gretchen Law.

January 9, 1987. Jane, Karen and I. Parked at Henon's. Walked to Chicken Hollow saltpeter cave. Lovely day. Looked at old mine shafts.

January 16, 1987. I painted kitchen, living room ceilings. Group walked front W Road to Doggy Hole. Jane Smith and Karen Stone.

January 23, 1987. Snowed Thursday. Jane could not walk, so in afternoon I walked to Edwards Point on road with Sally Wilbanks, Helen __, Inez __. Road trip 2 1/2 hours. Great views of distant hills and contour of ground.

1988

January 8, 1988. No walk - Snow

January 15, 1988. Nancy, maybe Jane, Jean. Met at Nancy's. Walked in woods, snow underfoot, to Rainbow Lake. Lunch on broken picnic table between old Girl Scout cabin and golf course.

February 5, 1988. Walked in new subdivision off Fairmount Road. Called on Mary Rankin.

February 12, 1988. Cold. Did not walk

February 19 - 26, 1988. Aspen

March 4, 1988. Home from Aspen

March 11, 1988. Walked on side of mountain to Watson's place (foot of Doggy Hole) then south under cliffs to new

house (empty) on high side Lower Brow Road. Lunch on a rock. Back to [Janice] Younger's.

Summer break

September 23, 1988. Nancy, Janice Younger, Elaine Hill, Jane, Marilyn, Jean. Met at Jane's house. Parked on Homestead Acres. Walked to power line brow, south to overlook - waterfall. Hot. Yellow jackets in the woods all day. First hike for Janice Younger and Elaine Hill.

September 30, 1988. Nancy, Janice Younger, Elaine Hill, Jane, Marilyn, Karen, Jean. Met here. Parked at Edwards' Point School. To Edwards' Point, 1 hour, 2.4 miles. Edwards' Point to Mushroom Rock, 2.5 hours. Mushroom Rock to School, 1 hour, plus lunch and rests. 10 AM to 2:45 PM = 4.75 hours. New trails freshly cut and painted. Pleasant day. Not too sunny. [See map on next page.]

October 1, 1988. Tennessee Trails drove from Nashville. Hiked from Signal Point to Highway 27. Graham [Hawks], Bob and I left cars at curve, Highway 27. Louie brought drivers back to Signal Point. Ken Dubke gave brief talk. 23 of us started at 9:30. Signal Point to Edwards Point 1.75 hours. Edwards Point to Mushroom Rock 2 hours. Mushroom rock to 27, 1.25 hours = 5 hours. This is walking time. Total time 6 hours. Estimate 7 miles, but I think it is longer. Two new bridges very nice. Met: Nancy, Peter, Andrea, Gene from Nashville. Met Colin and wife. Sasha girl from Woga Woga, Australia.

September 30, 1988.

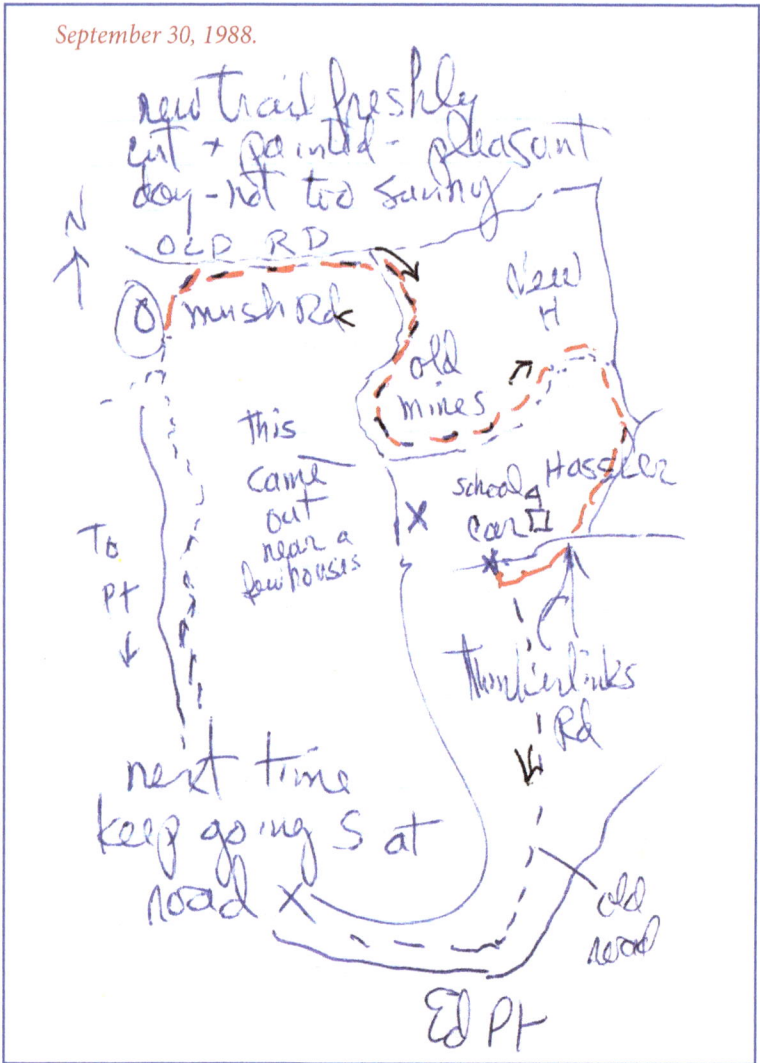

new trail freshley
cut + painted - pleasant
day - not too sunny

N

OLD RD

O. mush Rd

New
H

old
mines

This
came
out
near a
few houses

To
Pt

school
car

Hassler

Thunderlinks
Rd

next time
keep going S at
road X

old
road

Ed Pt

October 7, 1988. Janice, Jean, Jane, Nancy. Edwards Point School to Highway 27. Met men who planned to work on trail.

October 14, 1988. Reflection Riding: Janice, Elaine, Marilyn, Jean, Nancy. Six miles at least.

November 19, 1988. Tennessee Valley River Gorge Con. + Win Raoul, Ralph Brown – Riverview, Charlie Tucker, Graham Hawks, David - son-in-law of Jenson Nashville, Don Jensen, Chip Corley, Kathryn Phipps , Bob Phipps (broke leg), Jim Fitzpatrick, Lewis Pierce, John Smart, Jean Dolan. Met Red Food 7:30. Left parking lot at 8:10. Back to lot at 1:35 RAIN

November 11, 1988. Sarah [?], Marilyn, Janice, Elaine, Jane, Nancy, Connie, Jean. Chimney Rock – my birthday

November 18, 1988. Marilyn, Karen, Elaine, Ann Marie, Jane, Jean. Met at Henon's to Saltpeter Cave.

December, 1988. One day it snowed. Jane, Elaine and I walked to Buzzard's Point.

1989

January 6, 1989. Jane [Smith], Nancy [Moughrabi] and I walked to Brady Point from my house.

January 23, 1989. Marilyn, Jane and I walked to John Temple's lake. Beautiful noontime after terrible week.

January 20, 1989. Karen, Janice, Jane, Nancy, Marilyn, Jean. Met at Truex. Along Little Falling Water Creek.

January 27, 1989. Marilyn, Nancy, Janice, Jane, Karen, Jean. Met here. To Cleveland's. Walked to Redman property. Marilyn fell in [Shoal Creek.] Visited Elaine.

February 3, 1989. Nancy, Karen, Marilyn, Pam, Jean. Met at Jane's. Jake's - Pam's cabin for lunch. Watched men making shingles for Pam's cabin.

February 10, 1989. Nancy, Jane, Karen, Jean. History Museum. [Program was] Red Feather.

> *Be ye transformed by the renewing of your mind.*

March 10, 1989. All with Margaret [Popp?] to Huntsville.

March 24, 1989. Good Friday. Jane, Karen, Marilyn and I to old Anderson Pike. Lots of flowers. Cold. Damp.

March 31, 1989. Anne here. Dawn McCord, Marilyn, Janice, Elaine, Jane, Nancy, Jean. To Nature Center

April 7, 1989. Janice, Elaine, Karen, Jean. Snow – cold. Attempted to walk around Rainbow lake. Water too high. 3 hours.

April 14, 1989. No walk. I went canoeing with Peter.

Believe me, my young friend, there is nothing -
absolutely nothing - half so much worth doing
as simply messing about in boats

Grahame, 1908

April 21, 1989. Janice, Elaine, Nancy, Marilyn, and I walked from Covenant College to Nature Center. Approximately 5 miles. Beautiful day. Flowers. Hot.

April 28, 1989. Jane, Nancy, Marilyn and one dog. Wild flowers at W. R. Bend. Hot. Humid.

May 6, 1989. Marilyn, Janice, Nancy, Jane, Jean – wedding anniversary at Marilyn's. RAIN

Summer break

September 15, 1989. Janice, Jane, Nancy, Karen, Jean. Mushroom Rock.

September 22, 1989. Jane, Jean. Walked the Riverwalk. Rain.

October 13, 1989. Ridge west of North Suck Creek.

October 20, 1989. Tried to go to Blue Hole. Lost again.

October 26, 1989. Smith, Moughrabi, Younger, Stone, and me to Charit Creek Lodge [Big South Fork National River & Recreation Area, Jamestown, Tennessee]

November 3, 1989. Power Line Overlook

November 10, 1989. Astrid [Andrews], Connie, Jane, Janice, Elaine, Nancy, Jean. Blue Hole – got lost. – my birthday

> *Roads are for roaming more*
> *Than for arriving*
> *As life is more*
> *To be alive in.*

November 18, 1989. Snow. Sawyer Cemetery. I did not hike.

December 1, 1989. Elaine, Janice, Jane, Jean. From my house to brow through rocks and Allwood/Temple property.

Late December, 1989. Janice, Jane and I to Buzzard's Point.

1990

January 5, 1990. Maria [Lubkowitz] and I to Edwards Point. Light rain. By Cumberland trail.

Jean Blair Dolan

January 13, 1990. Nancy, Jane and I met at Fairmount Cemetery. Walked along Marshal Creek. DOG! Light snow – cold – lunch at old still site.

January 19, 1990. Nancy, Jane, Elaine, Jean. To Miller Cove Road. Walked down to Rock House Creek. Got lost. Ended up at pipe line on Suck Creek ___? Walked from 10:30 – 1:00 lunch; 1:30 at pipe line; 4:00 back at car. Very embarrassing. Don called Joe and he came looking for us. Lots of trail there to explore.

February 23 - March 9, 1990. Aspen.

March 23, 1990. Jane, Diane, Janice. Rain. (Rained out March 16 and March 30)

April 6, 1990. Elaine, Jane, Jean. Reflection Riding. Cold, rain.

April 13, 1990. Janice, Nancy, Jean to Henson Ridge. Met at Indyk Colvin's. Walked down creek. Good day.

November 2, 1990. Janice, Jane, Elaine, Nancy, Jean. Met at Janice's. Walked Watson's place.

November 9, 1990. Anne here. Rain.

November 16, 1990. Connie, Jane, Nancy, Jean. To Buzzard's Point. Connie brought wine.

69

November 23, 1990. Jane, Nancy. Jean. Walked under Signal Point to Alexian. Tired to find route to river. Hot.

November 30, 1990. Jane and I met at St. Augustine to Kay Gaston's and her mother's. Four of us met Nancy at Martha McCoy's. Walked her place. Had hot cider and fruit cake inside. She told stories. All except Nancy went. We ate lunch on a wall.

December 7, 1990. Linda Collins, Elaine (she drove), Nancy, Jean. Drove to Chattanooga Church Furniture [on Taft Highway.] Met Jane. Walked to Lewis Creek. Lunch on bluff overlooking creek. Jane's birthday; she brought wine. On way back I fell in the creek on my stomach! Total time from cars 3. 5 hours. Much destructive lumbering on top of old mines erosion.

> ***May God hold you in the hollow of His hand.***

December 14, 1990. Kay Gaston, Linda Collins, Jane, Nancy, Jean. Parked near Needle's Eye rock. Walked to Buzzard's View. Walked north. Lunch on outcrop. To Roberts Gap Road. Back on lumber road. Explored old cabin site half A of lean to. Back to car. Light rain.

December 22, 1990. Nancy and Jean. To North Chickamauga [Creek] to see paddlers putting in. Don Gray was one of them.

1991

January 4, 1991. Jane [Smith], Nancy [Moughrabi], Ann McKay, Janice [Younger], Jean [Dolan] to God's Rock. Then to Powerline cliff. Damp lunch south of waterfall.

January 18, 1991. Jane, Elaine, Janice, Nancy, Jean. End of Kell Road. South to above Connor Creek. Lovely day. Lunch at big overhanging ledge. Lots of shelters below and signs of digging. Nancy's birthday - wine and favors.

January 25, 1991. Elaine, Karen, Janice, Nancy, Jane, Jean. Elaine drove to Laudermilk's on Forest Park. Down Old Levi Gap Road to valley. New house with long drive. Back up. Pearsons have garden at bottom of escarpment and ladder.

February 1, 1991. Karen, Jane, Nancy, Janice, Jean. I was going to pick up Karen. I forgot but she found the wagon and followed us. Permission from Elizabeth Akins [then mayor of Walden.] Lovely day. Started at Loudermilk's. Under escarpment to Falling Water. Thick. Explored side trail. Went up a slot into a yard (Dr. Norton's) then down and hit old trail to under falls. Lunch in the sun. Back to Dr. Norton's; up through his side yard.

February 8, 1991. Elaine, Nancy, Jane, Jean to Prentice Cooper. Hiked from parking lot to Highway 27; 10 - 1:30. Explored Poplar Springs Camp Site. Ate on lovely overlook in the sun. Two cars - mine and Jane's.

February 15, 1991. Liz, Karen and I walked to first overlook at Edwards Point. Snow - later start. 1:30 - 3:40 P.M. Beautiful snow - thin. Cold 15º f. to 25º.

February 22, 1991. Aspen

March 1, 1991. Home but I did not walk. Believe they did the Redman property.

March 8, 1991. Elaine, Karen, Nancy, Jane, Jean. Snow. Buzzard's Point.

March 15, 1991. *Karen, Rebecca Garrigus ? (30 years), Elaine, Janice, Nancy, Jane, Jean. Karen's house start. Walked north to pipeline. Down and south under bluff. Fascinating. Comparatively easy. Three hours from pipeline to W Road. Found mark "Brown's 1981" on rock and stake. Rebecca fell and slid [part-way down talus slope.] Janice [accidentally] sat in the creek under [Cascade Falls] waterfall and walked back in [only] her black tights.*

March 22, 1991. Jane, Elaine, Nancy, Janice, Karen, Cynthia Cowan - Sierra Club member, Jean. To Edwards Point School, to Mushroom Rock, to bridge and return. Cynthia dropped knife in North Such Creek and retrieved it.

March 27, 1990. Mary Lou Fowler, Richard Halverson, Winston Crum, Jean. Walked under bluff to Falling Water Falls. Took short way out.

March 29, 1991. Good Friday - no walk.

April 5 - 6, 1991. Jane, Janice, Nancy, Elaine, Jean. Tennessee River Gorge Trust hikes. Hicks Mountain loop. Three hours including lunch.

April 12, 19 - No walk. Rain

April 26, 1991. *Jane, Elaine, Nancy, Karen, Jean. I drove to DeSoto State Park. We had Cabin 7. In afternoon we walked yellow - green trails along over bluff. Ate lunch in Picnic shelter. Light rain - to rain. Drove to Little River Canyon. Explored most of overlooks. Saw pinky red-white blossom _____. Helicopter will take junk cars from the ravine tomorrow. National Guard practice. (People drive cars over bluff after being stripped for insurance purposes.) Today was setting up. They lowered large receptacle while we watched. What a wind the copter makes. Good dinner salad, wine, bread, beef stew, banana pudding. We played Scrabble. Winner got choice of beds. We went in church. Back wall an enormous rock. Many couples married here. Saturday A.M. - Rain. Elaine left. We walked on yellow - green trails. Checked out. To Visitor's Center. Met two women from Rome who invited us to their cabin in Nimble Will Gap. Ranger showed slides and told us where to see pink lady slippers. We went. Saw 1000s. To DeSoto Falls; ate lunch; rain. Stopped in Mentone to see St. Joseph's church. Rain home 6:50 P.M.*

September 27, 1991. Nancy, Jane, Jean. Parked at Cowboy's.

Walked to Echo Point, top of Falling Water. Found old dug well and possible cabin site.

October 4, 1991. Karen, Connie, Jane, Nancy, Jean. Met at Nancy's. Toured her new handicapped access cabin. Parked at Signal Point. Walked to Brady Point and explored house under construction. 6500' finished floor space. Connie's birthday. She brought wine.

October 11, 1991. Jane, Karen, Nancy, Connie, Jane Frey, Joyce B. and friends, Jean. Connie drove to Boston Branch. Gloria Stewart let us in. We parked there. We started to Chimney Rock but kept turning right. Ended up overlooking outfall of Boston Branch Lake. Checked out Caldwell's cabin. Drove around Little Bend Road.

October 18, 1991. Nancy, Connie, Liz [Dolan], Karen, Jean. Middle Creek. Gorgeous day. Walked to St. Ives subdivision. Ate lunch overlooking lake. Back along creek to Bell's rocky lot. Saw Julian Bell. He said he gave McWhorter $10,000 to keep Town from getting Prentice Cooper property.

November 8, 1991. Karen, Jane, Nancy, Liz, Jean. From Homestead Acres to Powerline Overlook. Cold, light snow on ground. My birthday.

November 15, 1991. Elaine, Jane, Liz, Nancy, Jean. Five walked northwest side of Middle Creek. Beautiful.

November 20-21-22, 1991. *Karen, Jane, Liz, Nancy, Jean. Cabin at Pickett State Park.*

November 19, 1991. Linda Collins, Ruzia, Liz, Jane, Jean. Walked to little Buzzard's Point.

December 5, 1991. Parked at Jane's. Walked to Pam's. Met Tom [O'Neal]; went in cabin and house.

1992

January 3, 1992. North Chickamauga Creek upstream. Rain.

January 10, 1992. Five of us total. Met at Jane's. Short walk. Elaine parked at end of Gray Frier. Old coal mine.

January 17, 1992. Elaine, Nancy, Janice, Jane, Jean. Covenant college to Nature Center.

January 31, 1992. Elaine, Janice, Jane, Nancy, Jean. North Suck Creek.

February 7, 1992. Janice, Jane, Jean. Anne's birthday. Met at Younger's. Walked to Watson's platform and gate house. Saw first hepatica. Lunch at Janice's - wine, soup, bread and ice-cream. Janice's birthday.

February 21, 1992. I worked at Hunter.

February 28, 1992. Only Nancy and I walked North Chickamauga Creek to Spangler Farm. Lovely Day. Sierra Club called this 3 mile round trip. Found Corn Tassel Farm near Spangler Farm (Gone in 2000.) Explored nearby subdivisions.

March 13, 1993. *Most of group - Karen, Nancy, Jean (and some husbands.) To [Jane's husband] Joe Smith's*

*funeral at Wayside Presbyterian. [Burial followed at
Fairmount Cemetery in a family plot surrounded by
a wrought-iron fence crafted by Joe, who was a black-
smith and renowned fiddler.]*

March 19, 1992. With 19 Alexian Villagers to north Chickamauga Greenway. Left at 10:30. Ate lunch in Greenway
Shelter. Sun - rain, lightning, thunder - HAIL. We got
soaked. Took shelter at barn. To Spangler Farm. Saw Betty
Zander. Pete Snider took Susan and me back to bus. Picked
up group. Stopped at Corn Tassel Farm, miniature figures/
buildings on hill side. Home by 2 P.M. Hail did lots of damage on mountain.

March 20, 1992. Jane, Janice, Elaine, Karen, Jean. (Met
Wanda [Wilbanks].) To Nature Center. Walked to Spring
nearly 8 miles. Nice day. Steve Barry's come here to see and
talk with Jane.

March 27, 1992. Janice, Nancy, Elaine, Jean. To Hall Road.
Park 10 A.M. to Double Bridges (washed out 1982). Too
high to cross. Walked upstream following ATV path until it crossed though water. Turned back. Lunch at 11:30.
Downstream and up to car. Saw Mayflowers - waterfall - and
young man on ATV with 4-year-old on seat in front. With
car drove down Hall Road. Went in gate of old Leo Brown
place. Met young woman, Melissa Brown. (She said to all,
"You're Elizabeth Dolan.") Home by 1:30 P.M. (Melissa
Medford?)

Jean Blair Dolan

April 3, 1992. Jane, Elaine, Nancy, Jean. End of Kell Road

April 10, 1992. Elaine, Jane, Jean. Wanda Wilbanks (Met Wanda at Reflection Riding) joined us at Audubon Acres.

April 17, 1992. Good Friday. Jane, Wanda Wilbanks, Elaine, Nancy. I did not walk. Cumberland Trail.

April 24, 1992. Wanda picked me up; we got Nancy. Started walking 10 A.M. to Blue Hole 11:15. Lunch; feet in water. Picked up some trash. Saw pink lady slippers. Back to car 1:30. Slower uphill. Explored side outbreak of rocks. Home before 2 P.M.

Summer, 1992. Connie, Nancy and I looked at llamas. Walked back of Parry nurseries and to Jane's for lunch. Wine to celebrate Nancy's divorce. [Nancy reclaimed her maiden name, Clairmont.]

Summer, 1992. Connie Hawkins and I to Powerline Overlook.

Summer, 1992. Jane and I to Foster Falls.

September 12 - October 12, 1992. In Europe

October 16, 1992. No walk. Nancy and I looked at houses. [Nancy sells real estate.]

November 13, 1992. Jane, Jean. Birthday wine. Hike to little Buzzard's Point.

November 16, 1992. Hike to Powerline Overlook with Alexians.

December 11, 1992. Marion N. [Nentwig?], Jane, Nancy, Jean. Wine for Jane's birthday. Walked upstream Connor Creek. Met local house owner.

December 18, 1992. Elaine, Jane, Nancy, Jean. Buzzard's Point. We re-found old trail to valley.

1993

January 2, 1993 (Saturday). Jane [Smith], Maria [Lubkowitz], Jean [Dolan]. To Chimney Rock from Fosburg's - 40 minutes.

January 15, 1993. Jane and I from her place to Brown property. Cold - dull. Short walk.

January 24, 1993. Maria, Jane, Jean. To Buggy Top Cave with Randy. Too much water to go in but saw first hepatica. Left Signal 9 A.M. - home 3:30 P.M.

January 29, 1993. Nancy [now Clairmont], Jane, Jean. Met at Cowboy's to Square Hole. Wet, steep. Beautiful day. To Trillium Falls and straight up to Echo Point Wow! 10 A.M. (parking place) and return 2:00.

February 5, 1993. No walk. Anne and I in New England.

Jean Blair Dolan

Watercolor by Jean Dolan. Friends Pam and Tony Awtrey used it on their new year greeting card, writing, "This year's picture is from an old friend, Jean Dolan, age 97, former Girl Scout Leader of the women's section of the Ancient Scouts of North Atlanta. This is a group of then young boys and girls who 'scouted' together camping, hiking, canoeing, square-dancing in our teens … This year at Eastern Cape Cod. Jean and her daughter, Anne, came with us to the Cape.

From Rocks and Sand and Every Ill
May God preserve the sailor still.

February 12, 1993. On Saturday Maria, Jane, Gretchen, Nancy went to Savage Gulf. I did not go.

February 26, 1993. Marie [Braxton], Jane, Nancy, Jean. Snowed yesterday. To Nancy's for delicious lunch. Walked from Hidden Brook to Shackleford Ridge Road.

March 5, 1993. Jane, Nancy, Jean. Cold and dull. Near rain. To Hardy's [Restaurant] at 12:15

March 12, 1993. Nancy and I walked from end of Short Creek Road through Prentice Cooper to Blue Trail. Lunch under an overhang. Snowing lightly. (School out at 11, so Jane stayed to be with David, Amy's son. Snowed 13 inches on Saturday.)

March 17-18-19, 1993. Nancy, Jane, Liz, Cel, Jean. To Pickett State Park.

March 28, 1993. Jane and I walked with Randy to Souters Falls.

April 2, 1993. To Chattanooga State Technical Institute sculpture garden. Riverwalk and North Chickamauga Creek new loop. Rain and cold. Lots of wildflowers.

April 9 - rain; **April 10, 1993.** Jane and I with Randy to Stone Door. To Ranger Falls - 7 miles. 25 flowers in bloom. Dutchman's breeches. Beautiful day.

April 15, 1993. Jane, Marie Braxton, Nancy, Jean. To Reflection Riding. Cold, light rain.

April 17, 1993. *I went to Rainbow Lake. Someone chopped shrubs, trees. Boy Scout troop 254 setting up camp. I told them it was illegal. Three boys Boston Branch. Told them to leave a spotless site.*

To escape criticism:

Say Nothing

Do Nothing

Be Nothing

April 23, 1993. Jane, Nancy, and I to Kell Road. Beautiful. To Mike's Creek. In bloom: arbutus, foam flower, iris. Waded creek to North Suck. Lunch. Up bluff south of Serendipity Rock. 10:15 - 2:00. Much ground pine in woods near top of falls. Many more surveyor's marks.

September: I do not think we walked in September.

October 8, 1993. Karen, Jane, Nancy, Jean. Walk Flipper Bend from Homestead Acres. Met Britt, from Playhouse. March storm blow downs.

October 15, 1993. Karen, Jane, Nancy, Jean. Rainbow Lake. Downstream to Falls. Up to Alexian.

October 22, 1993. Connie, Jane, Nancy, Jean. Mushroom Rock.

November 5, 1993. Karen, Nancy, Jane, Maria, Jean. To [Sally Worland] Thomas' place [in McLemore Cove] in Georgia, Hidden Hollow. Gorgeous farm. Walked around 5 acre lake.

November 12, 1993. Jane, Karen and I to Middle Creek toward Lake. Birthday. Wine.

November 19, 1993. Jo Ann Peliteer (new hiker), Karen, Connie, Jean. From top of W to Morrison Springs [in the valley] by the old Corduroy Road [long abandoned route later replaced by the W Road.] Parked at Frizzell's. Saw Charlie's [Stone] new deck.

Cameron

November 28, 1993. Family. Cameron's [Anne's son] first hike. Anne and Jon, Peter and Sherrie, and I to Pot House loop. Rained.

December 3, 1993. Jo Ann, Nancy, Karen, Jean. To James [Boulevard] then Boston Branch and Chimney Rock. Gate card from Anne Caldwell.

~~ No records for 1994 ~~

1995

January 13, 1995. Anne [Dolan Driskill], Cameron [Driskill], Joanie [Sharp], Nancy [Clairmont], Helenna [Ordonez], Bunny [Sedgwick], Jean. Cowboy's to Falling Water Overlook.

January 20, 1995. *Nancy, Joanie, Helenna, Bunny, Jean. To Boston Branch. Light snow. To Chimney Rock. Tied piece of red tent [as a marker for identifying the location of Chimney Rock from the other side of the North Chickamauga Creek canyon.] Side trip to God's Rock. Cold.*

January 27, 1995. Nancy, Helenna, Joanie, Jane, Jean. Brady Point to Alexian and back on roads. Went in Mathis House. (Nancy had a lock-box key, but door unlocked.)

February 3, 1995. *Helenna, Nancy, Jane, Joanie, Pam, Jean. Met 10 A.M. Bowater [Pocket] parking lot. North Chickamauga Creek. Walked trail to 12 N (Up two flights of steps.) Could see red cloth on Chimney Rock!*

February 17, 1995. Joanie Sharp, Nancy, Helenna, Jean. Met downtown at Huffaker's [Realty.] Walked to Ross' Landing; gift shop aquarium; back Walnut Street Bridge. Lunch Mad Hatter. To In-town Gallery.

March 10, 1995. Nancy, Helenna, Bunny, Karen, Marie B.[Braxton], Jean. Connor Creek. Water high. Met at 9:45.

March 17, 1995. Bunny, Margaret Popp, Linda Triplett, Nancy, Marie Braxton, Jean. With Karen as guide, though back yards. Old log house. Natural bridge with bird [bas-relief dove carved in rock by Emma Bell Miles]. Lunch over waterfall. Warm.

March 24, 1995. Reflection Riding. Saw Shortia in bloom. Linda [Triplett] and I did rubbing of Emma Bell Mile's dove - off Altura Drive.

March 31, 1995. Linda, Marie, Jean. Met at pipe line on Shackleford Ridge Road. Walked downstream on Connor Creek. Cool. Barbed wire on north side of stream. Saw remains of old still. Axe marks on tank.

April 7, 1995. Bunny, Karen, Marie Braxton, Jane, Jean. Started at Baptismal Hole up Middle Creek and down other side and return. Saw trailing arbutus in full bloom - pink!

April 14, 1995.

and when Jane made noises into the silo
2 owls flew out.
We started to eate
12 — Bunny brot
birthday wine —
Afterward Jerry took
us all around the I.
we saw caves on tylouia
bank where the Nat. Ams
buried their dead.
Also saw Galloway cows
on   mainland.

Rachael the triplets dog was with us

April 14, 1995. *Bunny, Jane, Karen, Marie, Nancy, Jean. Roger Triplett had his boat. Jerry, Linda, Maggie and Walter Popp met us at landing near Baylor School (WDOD parking place) to Williams Island. Jerry member C. R. A. A. Well informed. Woodland and Mississippian Indians lived there. We saw deer, herons, and when Jane made noises into the silo, 2 owls flew out. We started - ate at 12. Bunny brought birthday wine. Afterward, Jerry took us all around the island. We saw caves on Tiftonia bank where the Native Americans buried their dead. Also saw Galloway cows on mainland. Rachael, the Triplett's dog, was with us. [In 1989, the State of Tennessee purchased the island; in 2017 it's known as Williams Island State Archaeological Park.]*

May 5, 1995. Bunny, Nancy, Marie, Karen, Jean. Drove to Grandview. Hiked up stream along creek. Found 2 stills on north bank. Found old road. Lunch 12:30. A big batch of pink lady slippers at lot 39. (SOLD to Robinsons) [Later the group would go back to find the lady slippers area completely destroyed by construction.]

September 13, 1995. Bunny, Helenna, Nancy, Jean. Nancy drove. Parked on Vandergriff. Walked toward Big Blue Hole. New graveled road. Crossing large shed.

September 20, 1995. Karen, Bunny, Jean. I drove to Vandergriff. Started toward Big Blue Hole. Explored new gravel road to right. (It goes to Layton Lane.) Saw large bull and

pony. Gorgeous day. Explored shed, 2 story made like pole barn. Giant timbers and telephone poles. There was saw-mill on site (now gone) in woods, a cookout and sitting area under a tarp. Old red truck. Leaded glass front door in crate broken on ground. Dog house and fencing stacked. Old road barricaded with sign "Wildlife Study Area - W.K." Whole shed area will be under fence almost to old chimney. Area cleared for house. Farm shed. We went straight east past old strip mine and pond across power line. Down to North Chickamauga Creek at Big Blue Hole. Time: left car 10:00. Down to Laymon Lane and back. Explored shed and walked; ate lunch. Left lunch site 12:00. At North Chick 1:00; sat on rocks. Left creek 1:15. Back at lunch site 2:00 P.M. At car 2:35 P.M. Several side trails old and new. As we reached mail boxes and to Laymon proper, 2 trucks Nashville Electric Power came out from where we had been. Poles that were not there last week were in place, but not all. The trucks must have been working in newly graveled area to left - where Karen, Nancy and I went in the snow last winter.

October 4, 1996. Nancy, Helenna, Jean. Parked on Shack-leford Ridge. Into school property. Tried to find old roads. All mixed with new. We met a foreman. He helped us find a start. We lost it. Through woods to old road to Mushroom Rock. Down to Connor Creek. Lunch. Up to soccer fields. Met Mary Decosimo Aho and Joanie Sharp on their bikes. Joanie needed first aid. Luckily I had Band-Aids and sponges! A nice day.

October 11, 1996. Only Nancy and I. Parked at Signal Point. 10:30. Down Cumberland Trail to ruined bridge. Heard voices. Met 3 women, Mrs. Wainwright and 2 sisters from Derry, Ireland, here for a birthday. The trail was more difficult than they expected; it's badly eroded. Back to our house by 1 P.M.

The day before October 10, Anne, Cameron and I walked from Wilderness parking area beyond Bee Branch (past old Girl Scout cabin) and Alexian.

1998

September 11, 1998. Bunny [Sedgwick], Chris, Nancy [Clairmont], Nancy [Fulcher],Cindy [Lamacchia], Jo Ellen, Ruth Ann [Kraft], Nelly, Jean. Edwards Point old camp site. Hot; clear.

September 25, 1998. Cindy, Ginny, Jo Ellen, Nancy C., Nadeem Moughrabi, Ruth Ann, Nelly, Jean. Guests Sherry, Michelle. Church of God to Mushroom Rock and bridge.

October 2, 1998. Chris, Cindy, Ginny, Jo Ellen, Nancy C., Nancy F., Ruth Ann, Jean. Falcon's Bluff. Robert's Mill Road toward Buzzard's Point. Too hot for me. Back to bluff.

October 9, 1998. Chris, Cindy, Ginny, Jo Ellen, Nancy C., Nelly, Jane, Jean. Pot House Loop. House was open. Sunny and not too hot.

October 16, 1998. Chris, Cindy, Ginny, Jo Ellen, Ruth Ann, Nelly and her sister, Jane, Jean. Maple Branch Road [previously knows as Chicken Hollow] to Lewis Cave. Mark trees with plastic .

October 23, 1998. Bunny, Ruth Ann, Helenna Ordonez, Jean. Kell Road to Mike's Creek to North Suck Creek.

October 30, 1998. Chris, Cindy, Nancy C., Nancy F., Ruth Ann, Jo Ellen, Jane, Jean. Guests Louise and Gladys. Cowboy's to lake to Sawyer Road. Ruth Ann's Birthday.

November 6, 1998. Cindy, Ginny, Jo Ellen, Nancy C., Nancy F., Nelly, Ruth Ann, Helenna, Jean. Guests Helenna and Gladys. Prentice Cooper parking lot to Highway 27. Perfect fall day. Jean's Birthday.

December 4, 1998. Bunny, Chris, Jean. Homestead Acres to Power Line Overlook

December 11, 1998. Bunny, Cindy, Jean. Guest Monita. Greenway Farm loop. Lunch on cabin porch.

1999

January 8, 1999. Chris , Cindy [Lamacchia], Jo Ellen, Nancy [Clairmont], Nelly, Pam [O'Neal], Jean [Dolan]. Windtree to Connor Creek and return. Rain.

January 22, 1999. Bunny [Sedgwick], Chris, Ginny, Jo Ellen, Maria [Lubkowitz], Nancy C., Nelly, Jean. Vandergriff Road to North Chickamauga Creek. Laymon Lane and return.

January 29, 1999. Chris, Ginny, Jo Ellen, Maria, Nancy F., Jean. Sawyer Cemetery Road to Buzzard's Point and return. Clear.

February 19, 1999. Bunny, Cindy, Ginny, Nancy C., Jane, Jean. Cowboy's to Falling Water Overlook.

February 26, 1999. Bunny, Maria, Nancy C., Nancy F., Pam, Jane, Jean. Bowaters to steps and return. Perfect day.

March 5, 1999. Bunny, Karen Stone, Karen Smith, Maria, Nancy C., Nancy F., Jane, Jean. Boston Branch to Chimney Rock. Cold. Karen Stone's birthday.

March 12, 1999. Bunny, Ginny, Karen Stone, Maria, Nancy, Nelly, Ruth Ann, Jean. Ochs Gate to Cravens House. Cool; clear.

March 19, 1999. Bunny, Maria, Nancy C., Nancy F., Jean. To Nature Center. Met Ed Bowers.

March 26, 1999. Bunny, Ginny, Karen, Karen, Nancy, Nancy, Pam, Jane, Jean. Grandview. Old Anderson Pike and return.

April 16, 1999. Cindy, Ginny, Jo Ellen, Karen Stone, Nancy, Nancy, Nelly, Pam, Jane, Jean. Sawyer Cemetery. Roberts Mill. Buzzard's Point. Nelly's birthday. Perfect. Nelly leader.

April 23, 1999. Bunny, Karen Stone, Nancy, Nancy, Ruth Ann, Jane, Jean. Maple Branch. Lewis Cave. Out south ridge.

May 7, 1999. Bunny, Cindy, Ginny, Maria, Nancy, Nancy, Nelly, Pam, Jane, Jean. Sue's trip near Johnson Spring. Met "Pete." Lunch at Sue's.

May 14, 1999. Bunny, Chris, Cindy, Ginny, Karen Stone, Maria, Connie Hawkins, Jean. Falling Water Creek to ? ? Leaders split. Reunited with glee. [As a result of this incident the group vowed never to become separated again.]

Ah !

Jean Blair Dolan

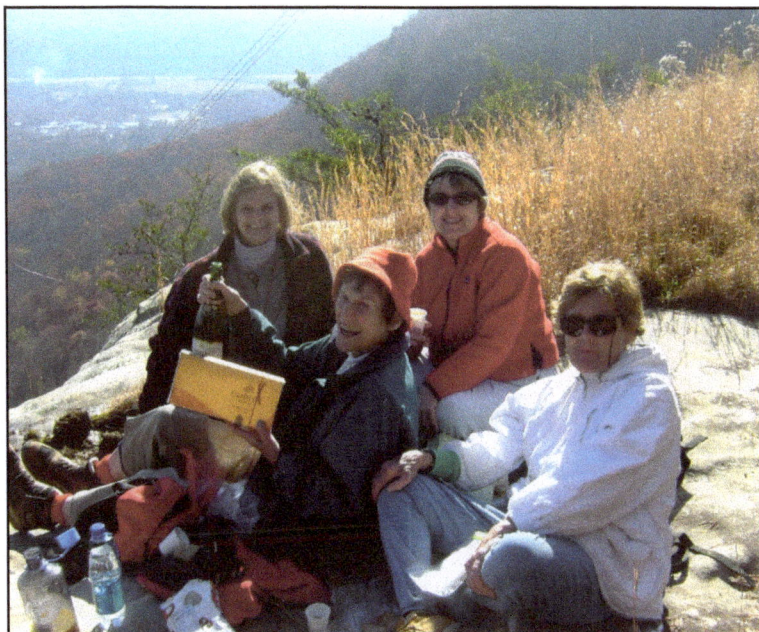

Jean Dolan's birthday hike with wine at Powerline Overlook in 2005. Left to right, Lynn Talbott, Jean, Nancy Clairmont, Connie Hawkins. Photo by Karen Stone.

July 19, 2001, in front of the Len Foote Lodge at Amnicola Falls. Left to right, Nancy Clairmont, Maria Lubkowitz, Bunny Sedgwick, Nancy Fulcher, Jean Dolan, with Karen "Narnie" Smith in front.

Jean and Karen "Pepe" Stone, Memorial Day 2015.

Jean Blair Dolan

Unfortunately the date, place and names of some of these hikers are not available. Left to right, Karen Stone, Jean Dolan with dog, _____, Bunny Sedgwick, _____, Lynn Talbott behind, _____, _____, _____.

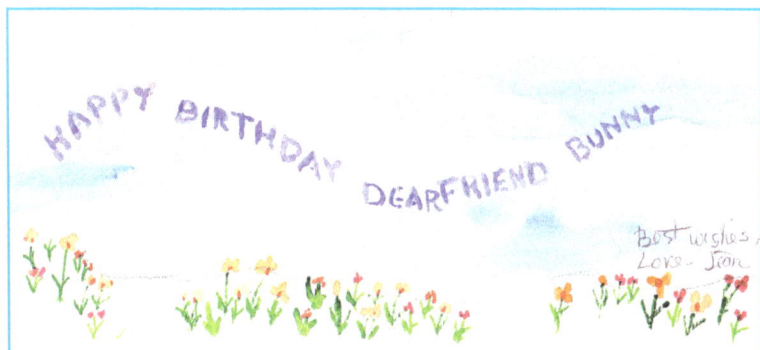

HAPPY BIRTHDAY DEARFRIEND BUNNY

Best wishes,
Love - Jean

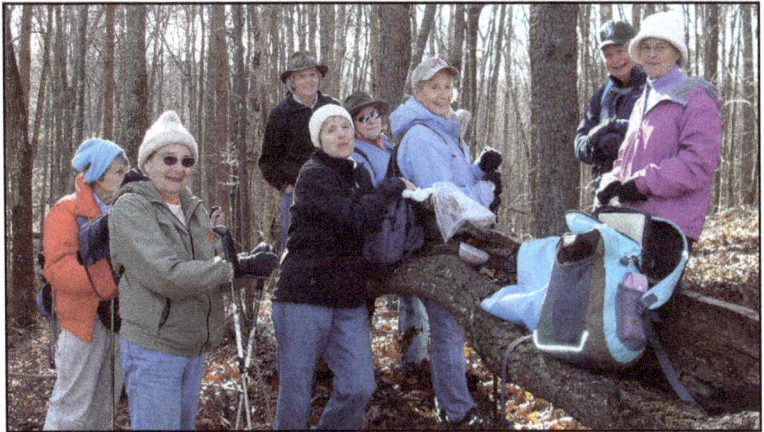

February 2, 2011, returning from Chimney Rock. Left to right, Jean Dolan, Jean Cook, Coyote Smith, Nancy Clairmont Johnson, Karen "Pepe" Stone, Gretchen Gugler, Ted Gugler, Karen "Mish" Gamble. Photo by Candy Smith.

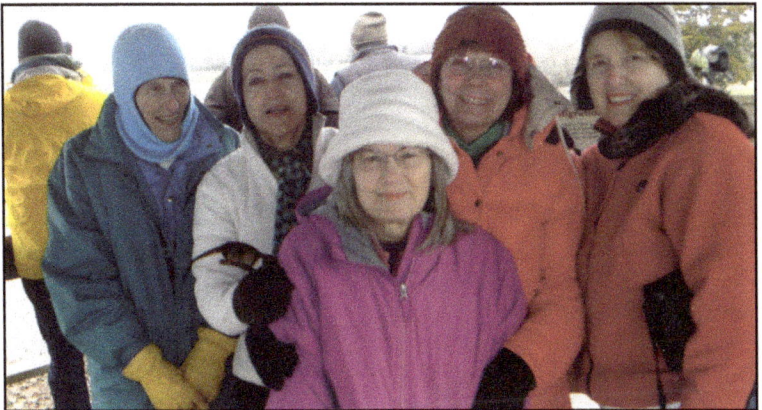

Winter 2012 at the Sandhill Crane watch on Chickamauga Lake. Left to right, Jean Dolan, Helenna Ordonez, Karen "Mish" Gamble , Karen "Pepe" Stone, Nancy Clairmont Johnson. Photo taken by Ted Gugler.

March 4, 2011, beside the remains of a very old burned cabin near Sawyer Cemetery. Left to right, Karen "Narnie" Smith, Nancy Clairmont Johnson, Karen "Pepe" Stone, Jessie Hutchinson. Photo by Jean Dolan.

Jean Blair Dolan

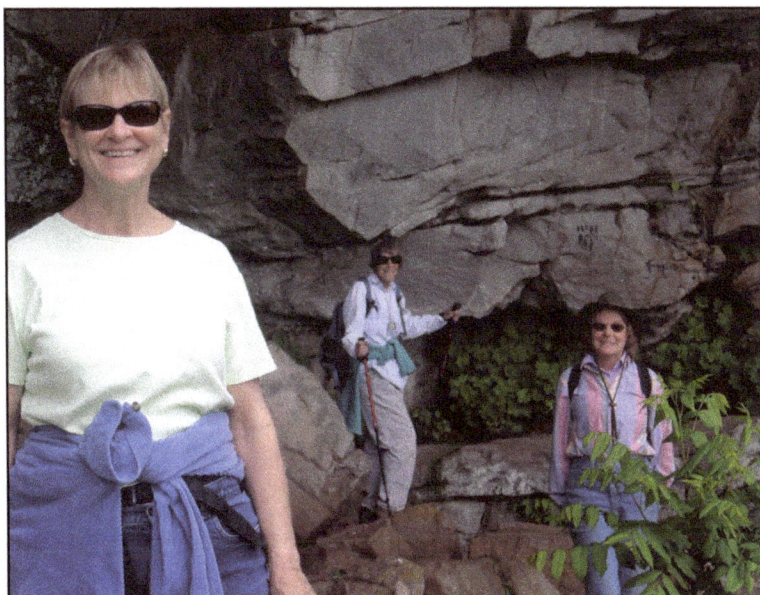

May 5, 2011. Exploring the great rocks above Falcon Bluff on the way to Buzzard's Point. Above these rocks on Sawyer Cemetery Road is "The Needle's Eye." Left to right, Mary Seay, Jean Dolan, Karen Stone. Photo by Jessie Hutchinson.

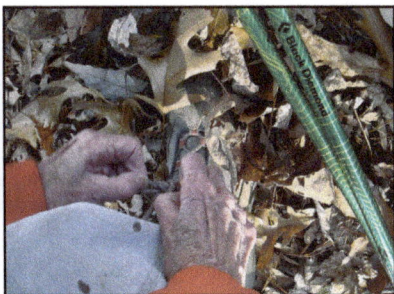

May 5, 2011. Jean at Falcon Bluff.

Any hike, any date. Pesky bootlaces.

October 10, 2012, on Turkey Trail, so-called because on the first hike there, we saw a wild turkey.

October 10, 2012, Nancy Johnson poses as if at the beach, since beaches come to mind when she sees beech trees.

March 15, 2013. Resting in the sun after exploring the high ground between Windtree and Boulder Point off Shakleford Ridge Road. Left to right, above, Gretchen Gugler, Jean Cook, Gail Bashnagle; below, Karen "Mish" Gamble, Nancy Johnson, Jean Dolan. Photos by Karen Stone.

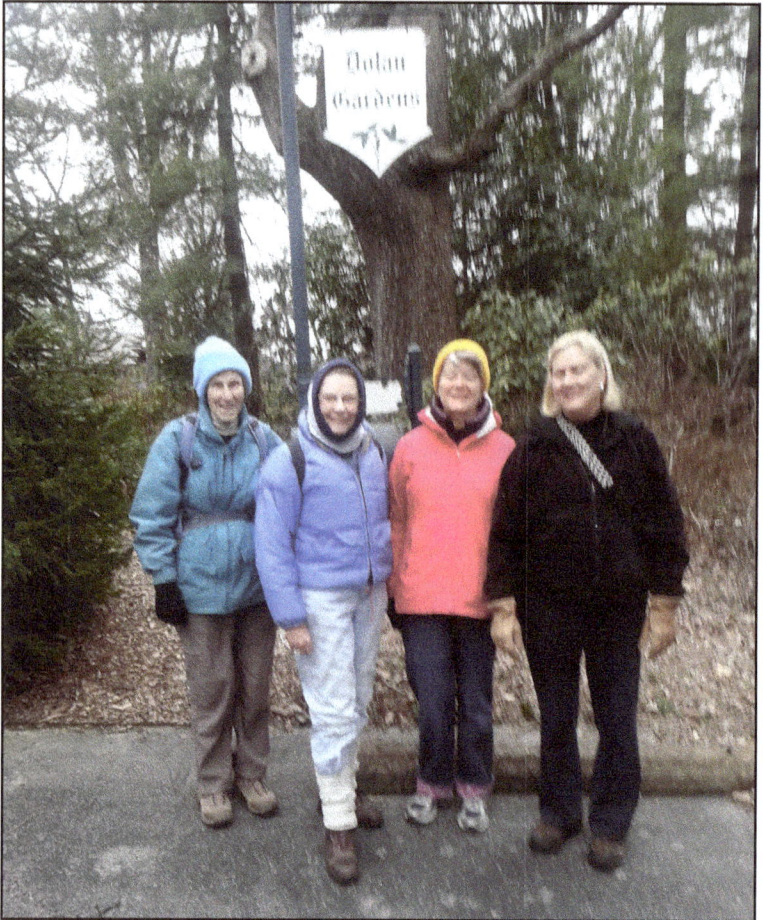

March 22, 2015, at Mrs. Jones' Garden on South Palisades. "Dolan Gardens" does not refer to Jean Dolan, but to Mrs. Jones' family name. Left to right, Jean Dolan, Karen Stone, Beth Weidner, Jessie Hutchinson. Photo by John Weidner.

April 12, 2015. Resting on the Welcome to Walden sign after hiking down the W Road to the first house, and picking up trash on the way back, left to right are Carolyn Longphre, Jean Cook, Gail Bashnagle, and Jean Dolan. Photo by Karen Stone.

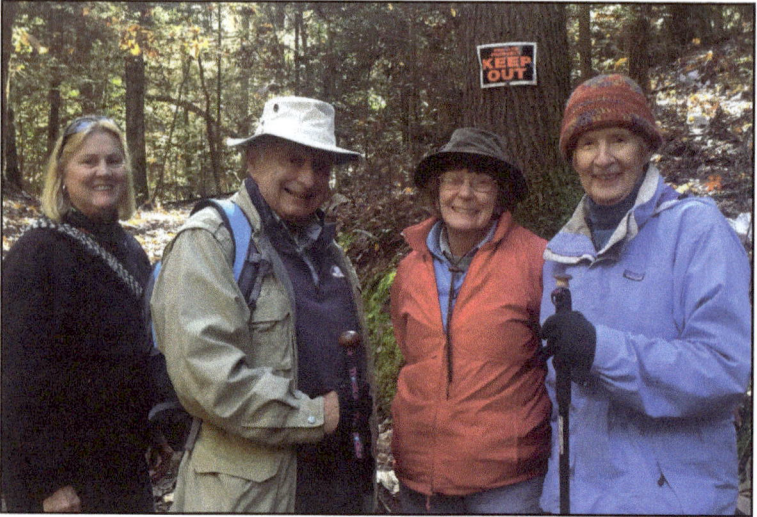

October 3, 2015. Posing in front of one of the "Keep Out - No Trespassing" signs we love so well. This one is on Pam O'Neal's property, which is called "Jake's" in many of the recorded walks. Left to right, Jessie Hutchinson, Ted Gugler, Karen Stone, Gretchen Gugler. Photo by Hilda "Bitsy" Horton.

October 3, 2015. Ted and Gretchen Gugler, Karen Stone and Hilda Horton. Photo by Jessie Hutchinson.

Jean Blair Dolan

At McCoy house after walking the trail, November 18, 2016. Hilda "Bitsy" Horton, Debbie Fassino, Carolyn Longphre, Jean and Karen Stone

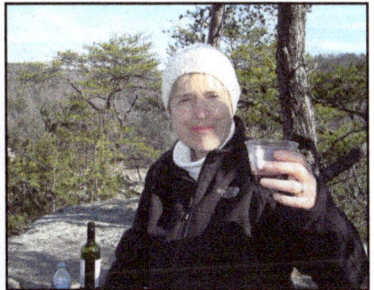

Beth Weidner, left, takes a break while Nancy Johnson offers some of her December birthday wine - 2013

June 2000
Buffalo River Arkansas (w/Tn. Valley Canoe Club)
Toney Pt. Campgrnd. 2 last nite. — TVCC

photographer → Kent Overbeek
trip leader
L → R.
    Clint Schmitt   Bill Hutchinson} married Nov '00
    Sherrie Dolan   Carol
    Mary Sutton   Becca Schmitt
    Pete Dolan   Carol Zitzow
    Julia   Lois Newton
    Jean Dolan
    Andrea Ford
    Karen Newman   ★ note: Buffalo Rvr. T shirts
    Louise Gilley   designed by Jean Dolan
                           for 30th trip.

At right, Jean is wearing
a T-shirt she designed to
commemorate the 30th
Buffalo River paddling trip
of the Tennessee Valley
Canoe Club in June, 2000.
Friends are noted above
as shown in the group
photo by Uwe Zitzow.

104

Jean Blair Dolan

Jean's children wish she would give THEM some of her paintings. At left with Jean are David and Anne Dolan Driskill. Photo by Uwe Zitzow.

Right, Jean at the Alexian Artists Exposition at the MACC in 2015. Photo by Karen Stone.

Jean, with Anne close behind, leads the pack on a walk at Reflection Riding. Photo by Uwe Zitzow.

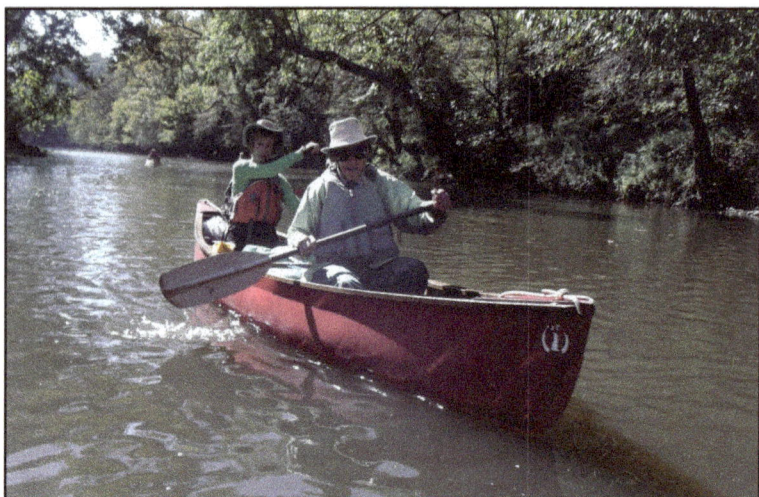

Carol Zitzow and Jean Dolan paddle the Elk River in the fall of 2013.

Jean Dolan and Buddy Wise take advantage of a lunch stop on the Elk.

Jean Blair Dolan

"In the fall of 2013 at age 97, Jean joined our Elk River overnighter trip on the Elk River, near Winchester, Tennessee. She was a super trooper, doing her part in paddling, setting up her tent, cooking and keeping us in such good company." Caption and photos of the river trip by Uwe Zitzow.

Jean with her trekking poles at age 101. Photo by Uwe Zitzow at Reflection Riding, November 2016.

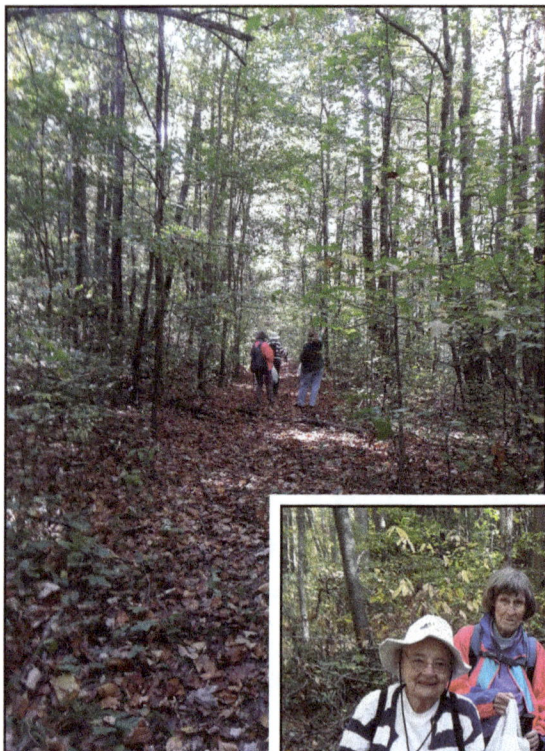

October 28, 2016, on beautiful "Coal Avenue," so named because it is still very obvious that it was a "real" road made broad and well enough for coal trucks to haul loads out from the end of Timesville Road. Jean Dolan, Jean Cook and Nancy Clairmont in the distance. Photo by Karen Stone.

Sometimes the trash we pick up can be recycled in useful ways - as in headgear. Photo on October 28, 2016, at Coal Avenue by Nancy Clairmont.

July 22, 2016, Carriage Ride at Reflection Riding: Jean, Nancy Clairmont, Jean Cook and Karen Stone. In another carriage that day were Anne Driskill, Carolyn Longphre, Jessie Hutchinson, and Gretchen & Ted Gugler

September 30, 2016, on the way to Edwards Point: Debbie Fassino, Karen Stone, Jean Cook, Jean Dolan and Carol Bishop. Photo by Nancy Clairmont.

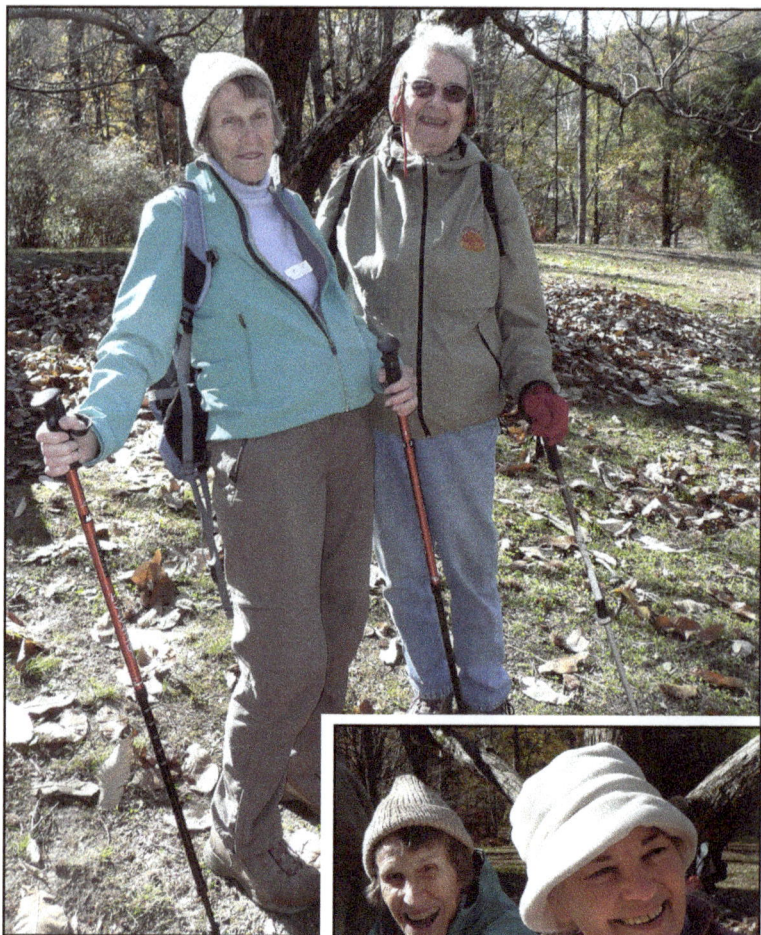

November 8, 2013, Reflection Riding. Jean Dolan and Jean Cook, above; Jean and Karen "Mish" Gamble, right.

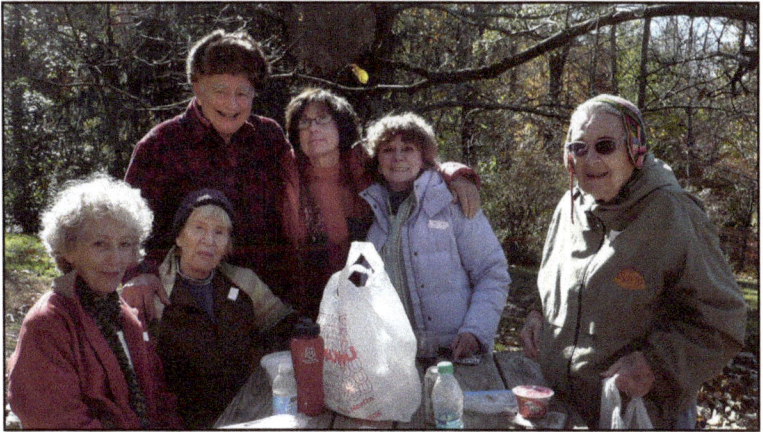

November 8, 2013, Karen "Narnie" Smith, Gretchen and Ted Gugler,
Carolyn Longphre, Karen "Pepe" Stone, and Jean Cook at Jean's 98th
birthday party at Reflection Riding. Photo by Jessie Hutchinson.

November 11, 2016, Maria Lubkowitz talks with the Reflection Riding
professional staff photographer. Jean Cook, Karen Stone, Jean Dolan and
Carolyn Longphre walk to the pavilion to celebrate Jean's 101st birthday.

99

November 8, 2014, celebrating Jean's 99th birthday at Reflection Riding. Left to right, seated: Ted Gugler, Karen Stone, Liz Seaborn, Jean, Gretchen Gugler, Carol Zitzow; standing: __, Daisy Blanton, __, Carolyn Longphre, Nancy Johnson, Mike Gaal, Karen Gamble, Bunny Sedgwick, Karen Smith, Jean Cook, Helenna Ordonez, Chuck Sedgwick, Coyote Smith, Maria Lubkowitz, Candy Smith. Photo by Charlie Stone.

Jean and Nancy Johnson enjoying birthday cards 2014

Jean celebrating 100 years of birthday greetings 2015

Ginkgo Angel Jean, 2014

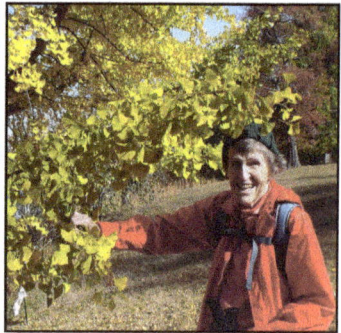

Ginkgo Enthusiast Jean, 2016

Jean Blair Dolan

100 Years *and counting*

Jean Dolan's 100th birthday on the 12th. Left to right, Maria Lubkowitz, Helenna Ordonez, Karen "Narnie" Smith, Nancy Johnson, Cel Noll, Harriet Hereford, Sherrie Liafsha [Dolan], Liz Seaborn, Linda Collins (back), Bunny Sedgwick, Jean Dolan, Hilda Horton (back), Jean Cook, Anne Dolan Driskill (back), Karen "Pepe" Stone, David Dolan (back), Rita Smith Irvin. Photos by Uwe Zitzow. On the preceding Friday's walk to Edward's Point on November 6, WTVC News Channel 9 interviewed and filmed Jean and the group as we walked. The piece was on television that evening.

101 Years

Jean is out of birthday wine already.

Jean Cook, Rita Irvin, Carolyn Longphre, Maria Lubkowitz, Karen Stone, Jessie Hutchinson, John Johnson, Jean and Nancy Johnson.

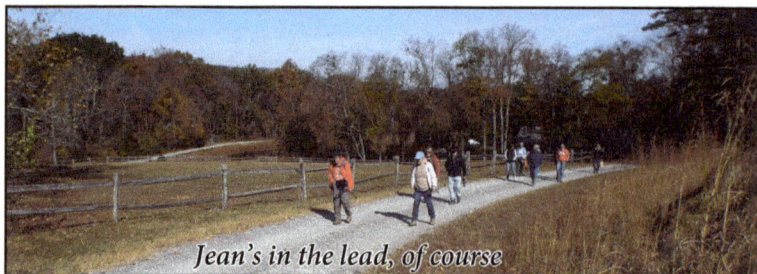

Jean's in the lead, of course

Jean Blair Dolan

November 11, 2016, at Reflection Riding celebrating Jean's 101st birthday. Left to right, Rita Irvin, Maria Lubkowitz, Carolyn Longphre, Karen Stone, John Johnson, Jean Dolan, Nancy Johnson and Jean Cook. Photos on this and facing page by Uwe Zitzow.

Jean, always way out in front, walks with John Johnson at Reflection Riding.

Random Memories
of some
Wonderful Walks

When I first started hiking, Jean was 65. She was talking about going in for a mammogram. It sounded like it was probably the first one she had ever had. I was young – in my 30's – and I had never had one. She was 65, and I thought she was so, so old. I couldn't believe she was hiking at that age.

I remember Jean falling in a creek. She slipped as we were crossing down below my place ["Jake's"]. The rocks are slippery down there. It was just Jean and I. We used to take a bottle of wine for our birthdays, but the slip in the creek didn't have anything to do with the wine. Jean used to come out to the farm every once in a while, and she would bring a friend for a picnic or a little walk.   Pam O'Neal

Once in the 1980's we went to Saltpeter Cave which is accessed by descending through a crevice in a rock face about 30 feet high. Down at cave level, we noticed some little naturally carved pockets that were round like igloos and would admit 4 or 5 of us. We crawled into one and sat in the cool, quiet, dark with our knees drawn up to our chests. Someone had a key chain with a small LED light, and she shined it onto dozens of dainty little spiderwebs in tiny rounded hollows above us. The light turned them a beautiful iridescent blue. It was magical.

Jean Blair Dolan

After leaving our hideaway, we continued along the cliff face. Nancy Clairmont heard rushing water ahead and led us to it. We found a lovely stream cascading down from the shelf above us. We decided to find another way up rather than heading back the way we had come, and we crossed the creek.

Soon we came upon the most frightening and shocking thing we have ever discovered on our hikes. A fully equipped, very old, campsite was abandoned under a small overhang. A nice wool shirt was on a drying rack beside a long extinguished fire. Pots and pans, food, shoes, clothes and sleeping bag were all there. One by one we each discovered some other item that indicated someone had left the campsite and not returned. When one of us found the man's shaving gear, comb and mirror on a ledge of the rock wall, we all panicked and wanted out of there fast. It was absolutely awful.

We scrambled on along the rock face and found a way up. We could not help but speculate all the way about who, what, why and when. Once above, we found an old overgrown road, and as we followed it toward our starting place, we came upon an abandoned U.S. Forestry truck. That freaked us out even more, and we rushed on toward our cars. Jean Dolan called the Forest Service and reported the vehicle. We never heard one more thing about the whole scary scenario. I wish we had. I will never forget that abandoned campsite as long as I live.

Karen "Pepe" Stone

Walking With Friends

We were in a great cabin at Charit Creek where we were all together in one room with bunk beds. It was cold, and our only source of heat was a wood stove. Jane Smith was the only one with experience with a wood stove, so she made a nice fire, and it was cozy when we went to bed. In the night, I dreamed I was burning in hell! Finally I woke up, and I was so hot I threw off all the blankets and stripped off my bedclothes. Jean Dolan was on the top bunk and she was burning up too. Fortunately Jane got up and fixed the fire, or we all would have died in that heat.

Nancy Clairmont Johnson

Jean and Gretchen [Law] had hiked out to Chimney Rock in Boston Branch and they hung a flag. Then the next Friday, they wanted to go to the other side and see if they could see it. We went up toward Soddy Daisy and hiked up the other side of the creek and we finally found it. We saw it. The leaves were off the trees so we could spot it. They were thrilled.

We had met a man named Sam who was living in a little house on Hixson Springs. He worked at Brock Candy Company. He knew all about the Boston Branch area and he agreed to hike with us and show us some things. We arranged to meet him, but he never showed up. The story was he had been having some words with a neighbor named Gadd, and Sam couldn't leave his house that day because the other man had held him hostage with a shotgun.

Pam O'Neal

Jean Blair Dolan

Gretchen and Ted Gugler, Karen Stone and I were walking at Mr. Ink's place which had been left untended for many years. We had been there when it was in its prime long ago, and we had enjoyed his wooded hillside of wildflowers.

This time, it was so much fun to explore the greenhouses. To find a plant, like a magnolia, growing out of a bottomless pot was precious. There was the plant growing without even any dirt, and it had survived somehow. It was especially surprising to find mountain plants, shrubs, and some things that had persisted there after years and years of neglect. And out back, alongside, and everywhere, there were rows and rows and piles of empty stacked plastic and crockery pots of every shape and size.

We headed out of the greenhouses to explore a part of the property where we had never been before. We crossed a little stream and lo and behold, a "host of yellow daffodils!" Long rows of daffodils had been planted by somebody, sometime. It was a wonderful mystery.

By that time we were really thirsty, so we traipsed back to the falling down old house and sat on the back concrete steps. We uncorked, consumed, and got tipsy on a magnum and two regular bottles of wine. It was Ted's birthday, and he had brought two bottles to share with what he thought would be a larger group. April 5th is my birthday, so I brought the magnum. Sitting there in the hot sun, drinking all that wine, made us feel really happy.

Carolyn Longphre

119

Walking With Friends

In the fall of 2003 or 4, Jean Dolan and I were walking alone on the trail from above Falling Water Falls toward Sawyer Road. Jean tripped on a root, went straight down on her face, and punctured her forehead with a rock. Head wounds bleed profusely, and we were both concerned that she might go into shock. However, she got up with the very calm demeanor you would expect, and we made our way back to the car on Sawyer without further incident.

We knew to get her medical attention, but Jean did not want to go to the emergency room. We sought aid from the pediatricians, the only doctors on the mountain at the time, but the receptionist said it was "illegal" for them to treat adults. Jean though I could just patch her up, and I was willing, but I wanted advice.

I called Dr. John Kington, a friend who had recently moved to the mountain and who I trusted for honest guidance. After ascertaining the extent of the cut by phone, he asked me, "How old is the lady?"

When I answered, "She's in her 80's," he asked if she were concerned about a scar. Jean said, "No," so he told me to take her to my house, lay her head on a towel on my kitchen floor, flood the cut with peroxide, and put on a butterfly bandage.

We did just that, and Jean ended up with no adverse effects except the scar she has to this day. From that incident our advice is – if you want to hike as a single pair, plan for all contingencies, and be careful.   Karen "Pepe" Stone

Jean Blair Dolan

We were walking one day when it was going to get hot, so we decided to head toward a creek where it would be cooler under the trees and rhododendron near the water. At lunch time we stopped to eat near a pool. One of the women, who will remain nameless here, decided to take a dip, so she stripped off all her clothes and went in. That might have been shocking enough to little conservative me, but it was a mixed group – there were some men along. She was hot and she wanted to get cool. That was all she thought about it. It didn't mean a thing to her. I will never forget it.

Maria Lubkowitz

I have often wished I were with the group on an occasion when they got lost. Sounds like a fun challenge to be completely befuddled for a while. There was a brief period of disorientation in some planted pines that all looked exactly alike behind Jane Smith's house. None of us could determine the way back to Jane's. We solved the problem by listening for cars on the surrounding roads and picking a direction to travel. It was fun solving that simple puzzle, and it was eye-opening that the wise and experienced Jane could get so confused even in her own back yard.

Karen "Pepe" Stone

One day we started out in my Land Rover headed down Brown's Chapel Road. There were about 14-15 people in that car, and they were hanging all over it. We had 3 on each side on the running boards. We were laughing because it was so

ridiculous and crazy. Some of the women we didn't know very well. Apparently they were worried about what we were doing and where we were going, and they kept making comments the whole time. One said to me, "You *are* Tom O'Neal's wife aren't you?" She was shocked. One moaned, "I should have gone to play golf today," and things like that. We wanted more than anything to get rid of those women.

You can go all the way down Brown's Chapel across to Suck Creek. We got to the creek and had to stop because I didn't know how to put the hubs on. But there was a man sitting there with a shotgun. He was one of the Lucky boys out there guarding the coal mines his father owned.

He said, "Well it's a good thing I w's here. I know how to do it." So he engaged the hubs and we went on. Our goal was to go 17 miles all the way out to the fire tower.

It was 1:00 and we decided it was getting late and we better eat lunch. While we were sitting there, all of a sudden all these men piled in with their tents and everything. It was the first day of hunting season, and we didn't know it. We abandoned the fire tower idea and went home with a whole car full of hollering women.

The next week, I think, we couldn't go into Prentice Cooper because of the hunters, so we went to Reflection Riding. Oh the mosquitoes were so bad. Somebody showed us how to take some sort of plant [Jewelweed] to rub on us to keep them off. That was interesting.

Pam O'Neal

Jean Blair Dolan

Once we were walking behind Jane Smith's house and we wanted to go to the creek. We were anxious to get there, so we just headed straight down the hill. The problem was, we didn't think about coming back up. I remember the bank was so steep I couldn't get my footing. The ground kept giving way, or sliding, out from under me, and I couldn't get a foothold.

Jane took a sapling - a little tree - and bent it over and down to me. I took hold of it and it gave me something to hold onto so I could scramble up. It didn't hurt the little tree, and I thought she was so smart to do that. She knew all kinds of things about the woods, and I always learned from her.

Another thing I learned was that Jean Dolan would cross any creek. She has wonderful balance. I might have been hesitant and afraid to get my feet wet or fall in, but she was an inspiration. She would just go across, and I remember her only getting a toe wet once in a while. She – unintentionally, of course – shamed me into following, and I found when I tried and followed her, I could make it.

Nancy Clairmont Johnson

Walking With Friends Is Wonderful

"What are these, Jean?"
"Why, those are L.B.M.s."
"What are L.B.M.s?
"Little Brown Mushrooms."

The End

Minion Pro on LSI 70# Archival white
Type and design by Karen Stone

Jean Blair Dolan

Notes